Fabulous

50 Crochet Bobbles, Popcorns and Puffs

by Jean Leinhauser

Leisure Arts, Inc.
Little Rock, Arkansas

Produced by

Production Team

Creative Directors: Jean Leinhauser and
Rita Weiss

Managing Editor: Mary Ann Frits

Senior Technical Editor: Ellen W. Liberles

Photographer: Carol Wilson Mansfield

Pattern Tester: Tammy Layte

Book Design: Linda Causee

Published by Leisure Arts

©2012 by Leisure Arts, Inc.,
5701 Ranch Drive
Little Rock, AR 72223
www.leisurearts.com

Introduction

Part of the fun of crocheting is finding and experimenting with new types of stitches. If you've never added texture and embossing to your crocheting, now is the time to learn how to add bobbles, popcorns and puffs to your work.

This book is a collection of 50 fabulous stitches which you can use in many different ways—for afghans, for sweaters, for hats, for baby items—for anything you might want to crochet with your hooks.

You're not going to find any mention here of gauge. That's because you can crochet these stitches with any type or size of yarn you choose—from bulky to the finest lace weight thread. The project will look quite different depending on the yarn you choose.

What you will find here are the words "chain multiple" at the start of each pattern given like this: "Chain multiple: 6 + 4." A multiple is the number of chains needed to work one complete unit of a pattern. In the example (6 + 4), to work the pattern you need to chain any number of stitches which can be divided evenly by 6: 12, 24, 36, etc. To this number you need to add 4 more chains giving a total of 16, 22, 28, 40, etc. The "+" number is added just once.

Have fun making swatches with these patterns, then pick your favorites and begin creating new and exciting projects.

Contents

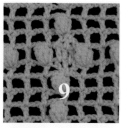
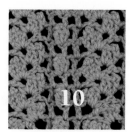
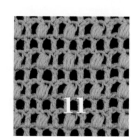
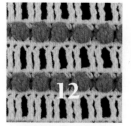

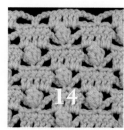
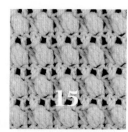
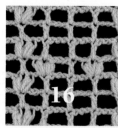
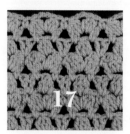
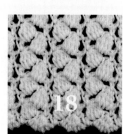

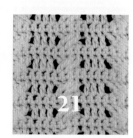

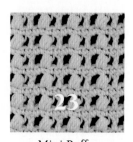
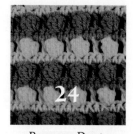
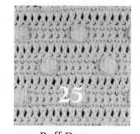
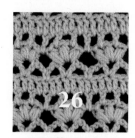
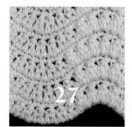

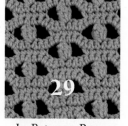
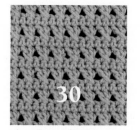
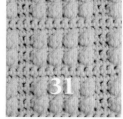

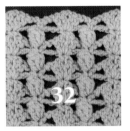

Treasures

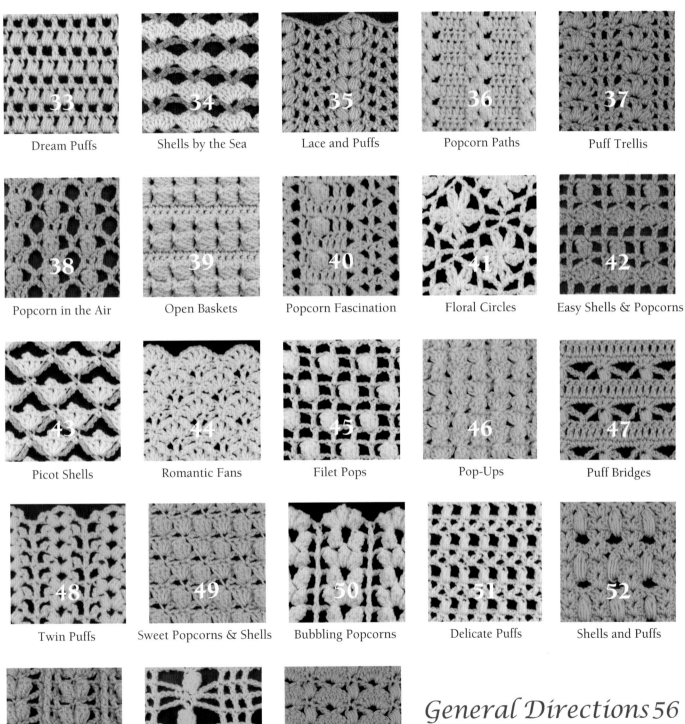

33 Dream Puffs	**34** Shells by the Sea	**35** Lace and Puffs	**36** Popcorn Paths	**37** Puff Trellis
38 Popcorn in the Air	**39** Open Baskets	**40** Popcorn Fascination	**41** Floral Circles	**42** Easy Shells & Popcorns
43 Picot Shells	**44** Romantic Fans	**45** Filet Pops	**46** Pop-Ups	**47** Puff Bridges
48 Twin Puffs	**49** Sweet Popcorns & Shells	**50** Bubbling Popcorns	**51** Delicate Puffs	**52** Shells and Puffs
53 Popcorns and Posts	**54** Popcorn Columns	**55** Linked Puffs and Shells		

General Directions 56

Diamond Popcorns

Chain multiple: 12 + 6

STITCH GUIDE

Bobble (bobble): Keeping last lp of each tr on hook, 3 tr in specified sp; yo, draw through all 4 lps on hook: bobble made.

Instructions

Row 1 (wrong side): Sc in 2nd ch from hook and in next ch, *ch 1, sk next ch, sc in each of next 5 chs, rep from * to last 3 chs, ch 1, sk next ch, sc in each of next 2 chs; ch 2 (counts as first dc on following rows), turn.

Row 2 (right side): Dc in next sc, *ch 1, sk next ch-1 sp, dc in each of next 5 sc; rep from * across to last ch-1 sp, ch 1, sk last ch-1 sp, dc in each of last 2 sc; ch 1, turn.

Note: *On following row, push bobble to right side.*

Row 3: Sc in first 2 dc, *bobble in next ch-1 sp on 2nd row below, on working row, sc in next dc, ch 1, sk next dc, sc in next 3 dc, bobble in next ch-1 sp on 2nd row below, on working row, sc in next 3 dc, ch 1, sk next dc, sc in next dc; rep from * to last ch-1 sp on 2nd row below, bobble in last ch-1 sp on 2nd row below, sc in next dc and in 2nd ch of turning ch-2, ch 2; turn.

Row 4: Dc in next 3 sts, *ch 1, sk next ch-1 sp, dc in next 7 sts, ch 1, sk next ch-1 sp, dc in next 3 sts; rep from * to last sc, dc in last sc; ch 1, turn.

Row 5: Sc in first 4 dc, *bobble in next ch-1 sp on 2nd row below, on working row, sc in next dc, ch 1, sk next dc, sc in next 3 dc, ch 1, sk next dc, sc in next dc, bobble in next ch-1 sp on 2nd row below, on working row, sc in next 3 dc; rep from * to turning ch-2, sc in 2nd ch of turning ch-2; ch 2, turn.

Row 6: Dc in next 5 sts, *ch 1, sk next ch-1 sp, dc in next 3 sts, ch 1, sk next ch-1 sp**, dc in next 7 sts; rep from * ending last rep at **, dc in next 6 sts; ch 1, turn.

Row 7: Sc in first 6 dc, *bobble in next ch-1 sp on 2nd row below, on working row, sc in next dc, ch 1, sk next dc, sc in next dc, bobble in next ch-1 sp on 2nd row below, on working row, sc in next 3 dc**, ch 1, sk next dc, sc in next 3 dc; rep from * ending last rep at **, sc in next 2 dc and in 2nd ch of turning ch-2; ch 2, turn.

Row 8: Dc in next 7 sts, *ch 1, sk next ch-1 sp, dc in next 5 sc; rep from * to last 3 sts, dc in last 3 sts; ch 1, turn.

Row 9: Sc in first 6 dc, ch 1, sk next dc, sc in next dc, *bobble in next ch-1 sp on 2nd row below, on working row, sc in next dc, ch 1, sk next dc, sc in next 3 dc**, bobble in next ch-1 sp on 2nd row below, on working row, sc in next 3 dc, ch 1, sk next dc, sc in next dc; rep from * ending last rep at **, sc in next 2 dc and in 2nd ch of turning ch-2; ch 2, turn.

Row 10: Rep row 6.

Row 11: Sc in first 4 dc, *ch 1, sk next dc, sc in next dc, bobble in next ch-1 sp on 2nd row below, on working row, sc in next 3 dc, bobble in next ch-1 sp on 2nd row below, on working row, sc in next dc, ch 1, sk next dc, sc in next 3 dc; rep from * to turning ch-2, sc in 2nd ch of turning ch-2; ch 2, turn.

Row 12: Rep row 4.

Row 13: Sc in first 2 dc, ch 1, sk next dc, sc in next dc, *bobble in next ch-1 sp on 2nd row below, on working row, sc in next 3 dc, ch 1, sk next dc, sc in next 3 dc, bobble in next ch-1 sp on 2nd row below, on working row, sc in next dc, ch 1, sk next dc, sc in next dc; rep from * to turning ch-2, sc in 2nd ch of turning ch-2; ch 2, turn.

Row 14: Dc in next sc, *ch 1, sk next ch-1 sp, dc in next 5 sts; rep from * across to last ch-1 sp, ch 1, sk last ch-1 sp, dc in last 2 sc; ch 1, turn.

Row 15: Sc in first 2 dc, *bobble in next ch-1 sp on 2nd row below, on working row, sc in next dc, ch 1, sk next dc, sc in next 3 dc, bobble in next ch-1 sp on 2nd row below, on working row, sc in next 3 dc, ch 1, sk next dc, sc in next dc; rep from * to last ch-1 sp on 2nd row below, bobble in last ch-1 sp on 2nd row below, sc in next dc and in 2nd ch of turning ch-2; ch 2, turn.

Repeat Rows 4-15 for pattern. At end of last row, do not ch or turn; finish off.

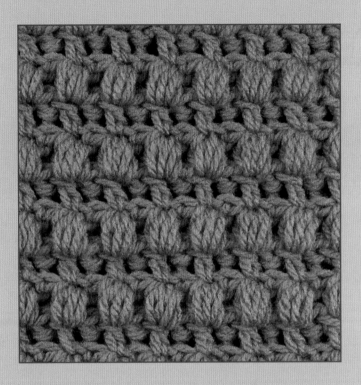

Little Puffs in a Row

Chain multiple: 2

STITCH GUIDE

Puff St (Pst): (YO, insert hook into specified st and draw up a lp to height of a dc) 4 times; YO and draw through all 9 lps on hook: Pst made

Front Post double crochet (FPdc): YO, insert hook from front to back to front around post (vertical bar) of specified st and draw up a lp; (YO and draw through 2 lps on hook) twice: FPdc made.

Back Post double crochet (BPdc): YO, insert hook from back to front to back around post (vertical bar) of specified st and draw up a lp; (YO and draw through 2 lps onhook) twice: BPdc made.

Instructions

Row 1: Sc in 2nd ch from hook and in each rem ch; ch 3 (counts as first dc on following row), turn.

Row 2: Dc in each sc across; ch 3, turn.

Row 3: *Pst in next dc, FPdc around next dc; rep from * across to last 2 sts, Pst in next dc, dc in last st; ch 3, turn.

Row 4 (right side): *Dc in top of next Pst, BPdc around next FPdc; rep from * across to last 2 sts, dc in top of next Pst, dc in last st; ch 3, turn.

Repeat Rows 3 and 4 for pattern. At end of last row, do not ch or turn; finish off.

Fence Puffs

Chain multiple: 4 + 2

STITCH GUIDE

Puff Stitch (Pst): (YO insert hook into specified st and draw up a lp to height of a dc) 3 times; YO and draw through all 7 lps on hook; ch 1: Pst made.

Front Post triple crochet (FPtr): YO twice; insert hook from front to back to front around post (vertical bar) of specified st; (YO and draw through 2 lps) 3 times: FPtr made.

Back Post triple crochet (BPtr): YO twice; insert hook from back to front to back around post (vertical bar) of specified st; (YO and draw through 2 lps) 3 times: BPtr made.

Instructions

Row 1 (wrong side): Sc in 2nd ch from hook and in each rem ch; ch 3 (counts as first dc on following rows), turn.

Row 2 (right side): Dc in each st across; ch 3, turn.

Row 3: *BPtr around next st, Pst in next st, BPtr around next st, dc in next st; rep from * across; ch 3, turn.

Row 4: FPtr around next BPtr, dc in next Pst; *FPtr around next BPtr, dc in next dc, FPtr around next BPtr, dc in next Pst; rep from * across, ending last rep with FPtr around last BPtr, dc in last dc; ch 3, turn.

Repeat Rows 3 and 4 for pattern. At end of last row, do not ch or turn; finish off.

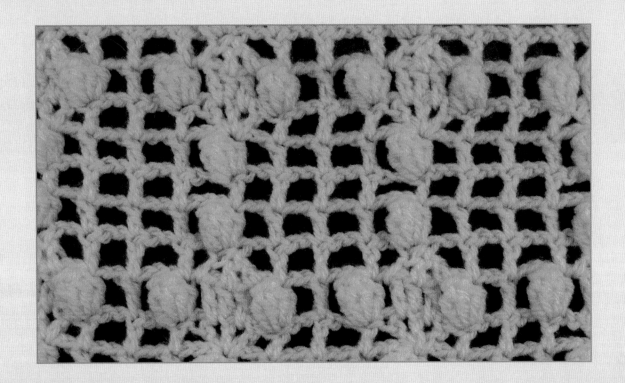

Popcorn Triangles

Chain multiple: 12 + 5

STITCH GUIDE

Popcorn (PC): Work 5 dc in specified st; drop lp from hook, insert hook from front to back in top of first dc made, insert hook in dropped lp and draw through, ch 1: PC made.

Shell: In specified st work (dc, ch 1) twice, dc in same st: shell made.

Instructions

Row 1 (wrong side): Dc in 4th ch from hook (beg 3 skipped chs count as a dc); *ch 2, skip next 2 chs, dc in next ch; rep from * across to last 4 chs, ch 2, skip next 2 chs, dc in last 2 chs; ch 3 (counts as first dc on following rows), turn.

Row 2 (right side): PC in next dc; *(ch 2, dc in next dc) 3 times**; ch 2, PC in next dc; rep from * across, ending last rep at **; ch 2, PC in next dc, dc in top of turning ch; ch 3, turn.

Row 3: (Dc, ch 1, dc) in top of next PC; *(dc in next dc, ch 2) twice, dc in next dc**; shell in next PC; rep from * across, ending last rep at **; in top of last PC work (dc, ch 1, dc), dc in 3rd ch of turning ch-3; ch 3, turn.

Row 4: Dc in next dc and in next ch-1 sp, ch 1, skip next dc; *PC in next dc, ch 2, dc in next dc, ch 2, PC in next dc, ch 1, dc in next ch-1 sp, dc in next dc**; dc in next ch-1 sp, ch 1, skip next dc; rep from * across, ending last rep at **, then dc in 3rd ch of turning ch-3; ch 3, turn.

Row 5: YO, insert hook in next dc and draw up a lp; YO and draw through 2 lps; YO, insert hook in next ch-1 sp and draw up a lp; YO and draw through 2 lps; YO and draw through 3 lps: half CL made; *ch 2, dc in next PC, ch 2, dc in next dc, ch 2**, dc in next PC, ch 2; YO, insert hook in next ch 1 sp and draw up a lp, YO and draw through 2 lps; YO, skip next dc, insert hook in next dc and draw up a lp, YO and draw through 2 lps; YO, insert hook in next ch-1 sp and draw up a lp, YO and draw through 2 lps; YO and draw through all 4 lps on hook: CL made; rep from * across, ending last rep at **, dc in last PC, ch 2, YO, insert hook in next next ch-1 sp, YO and draw up a lp, YO and draw through 2 lps, YO, insert hook in last dc and draw up a lp, YO and draw through 2 lps, YO and draw through 3 lps: half CL made; dc in 3rd ch of turning ch-3; ch 3, turn.

Row 6: PC in top of next half CL; *(ch 2, dc in next dc) 3 times, ch 2**, PC in top of next CL; rep from * across, ending last rep at **; PC in top of last half CL, dc in 3rd ch of turning ch-3; ch 3, turn.

Row 7: Dc in top of next PC; *(ch 2, dc in next dc) 3 times, ch 2, dc in top of next PC; rep from * across, ending last rep with dc in 3rd ch of turning ch-3; ch 3, turn.

Repeat Rows 2 through 7. At end of last row, do not ch or turn; finish off.

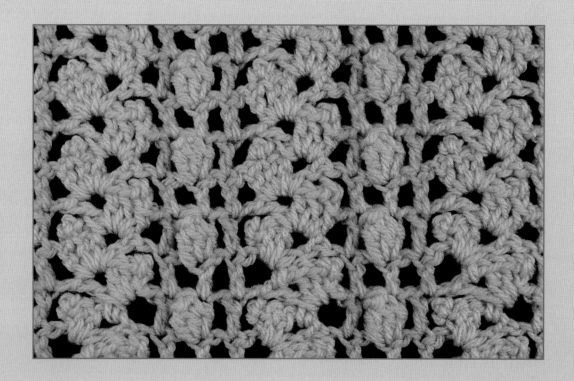

Picots and Popcorns

Chain multiple: 14 + 5

STITCH GUIDE

Picot: Ch 3, sl st in base of ch: picot made.

Shell: In same st or sp work (dc, picot, 2 dc, ch 2, dc): shell made.

Popcorn (PC): Work 4 dc in specified st; drop lp from hook, insert hook from front to back in top of first dc made, hook dropped lp and draw through: PC made.

Instructions

Row 1 (right side): Dc in 7th ch from hook; *ch 1, skip next 4 chs, shell in next ch; ch 1, skip next 4 chs**; dc in next ch, ch 1, skip next ch; PC in next ch; ch 1, skip next ch, dc in next ch; rep from * across, ending last rep at **; dc in next ch, ch 1, skip next ch, dc in last ch; ch 4 (counts as a dc and ch-1 sp on following rows), turn.

Row 2: Dc in next dc; *ch 1, shell in ch-2 sp of next shell, ch 1**, dc in next dc; ch 1, dc in next PC, ch 1, dc in next dc; rep from * across, ending last rep at **; dc in next dc, ch 1, dc in 3rd ch of turning ch; ch 4, turn.

Row 3: Dc in next dc; *ch 1, shell in ch-2 sp of next shell, ch 1, dc in next dc; ch 1**, PC in next dc, ch 1, dc in next dc; rep from * across, ending last rep at **; dc in 3rd ch of turning ch-4; ch 4.

Repeat Rows 2 and 3 for pattern. At end of last row, do not ch or turn; finish off.

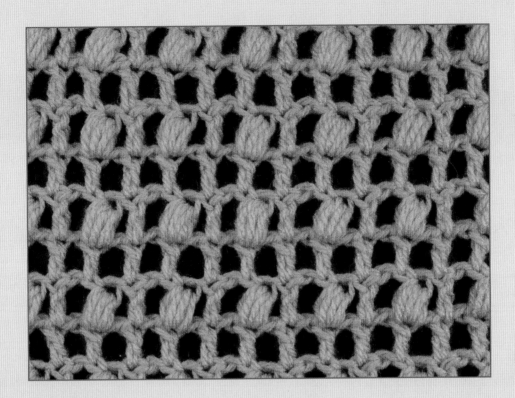

Dancing Puffs

Chain multiple: 4+2

STITCH GUIDE

Puff Stitch (PS): (YO, insert hook into specified st and draw up a lp to height of a dc) 4 times; YO and draw through all 9 lps on hook: PS made.

Instructions

Row 1 (wrong side): Sc in 2nd ch from hook and in each rem ch; ch 4 (counts as first dc and ch-1 sp on following rows), turn.

Row 2 (right side): Skip next sc, dc in next sc; *ch 1, skip next sc, dc in next sc; rep from * across; ch 4, turn.

Row 3: PS in next dc; *ch 1, dc in next dc, ch 1, PS in next dc; rep from * across to turning ch; ch 1, dc in 3rd ch of turning ch-3; ch 4, turn.

Row 4: Dc in top of next PS, ch 1, *dc in next dc, ch 1, dc in top of next PS, ch 1; rep from * across to turning ch; dc in 3rd ch of turning ch-3; ch 4, turn.

Repeat Rows 3 and 4 for pattern. At end of last row, do not ch or turn. Finish off.

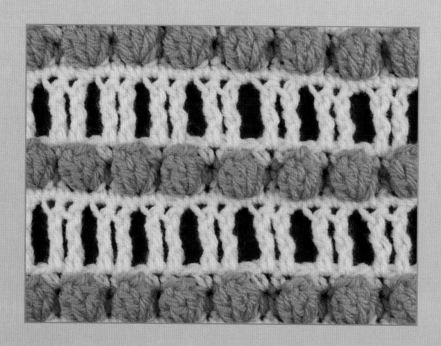

Playful Popcorns

Chain multiple: 3

Two Colors: color A and color B

STITCH GUIDE

Popcorn Stitch (PC): Work 5 dc in specified st; drop lp from hook, insert hook from front to back in top of first dc worked, insert hook in dropped lp and draw through, ch 1; PC made.

Instructions

Work beg ch with color A.

Row 1 (right side): With color A, sc in 2nd ch from hook and in each rem ch; ch 4 (counts as first tr on following rows), turn.

Row 2: Tr in next sc; *ch 1, skip next sc, tr in each of next 2 sc; rep from * across, ch 1, turn.

Row 3 (right side): Sc in each tr and ch-1 sp across; finish off color A. Do not turn.

Row 4 (right side): With right side facing, join color B with sc in first sc at right; sc in next st; *PS in next st, sc in each of next 2 sts; rep from * across. Finish off color B. Do not turn.

Row 5 (right side): Join color A with sc in first sc at right, sc in next st; *ch 1, skip next PS, sc in each of next 2 sts; rep from * across; ch 4, turn.

Row 6: Tr in next sc; *ch 1, skip ch-1 over next PS, tr in each of next 2 sts; rep from * across, ch 1, turn.

Row 7 (right side): Sc in each st and in each ch-1 sp across. Finish off color A. Do not turn.

Repeat Rows 4 through 7 for pattern. At end of last row, do not ch or turn; finish off.

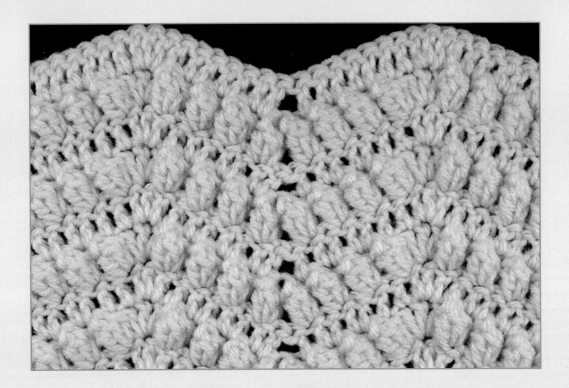

Ripple Popcorns

Chain multiple: 17 + 2

STITCH GUIDE

Popcorn (PC): Work 4 dc in specified st; drop lp from hook, insert hook from front to back through top of first dc made, insert hook in dropped lp and draw through lp on hook: PC made.

Dec in 2 dc: (YO and draw up lp in next dc, YO and draw through first 2 lps on hook) twice, YO and draw through all 3 lps on hook.

Instructions

Row 1 (right side): Dc in 4th ch from hook (beg 3 skipped chs count as a dc) and in each of next 6 chs; *3 dc in next ch; dc in each of next 7 chs, sk next 2 chs, dc in each of next 7 chs; rep from * across to last 9 chs, 3 dc in next ch, dc in each of next 8 chs; ch 2, turn. (Ch-2 does not count as st on following rows.)

Row 2: Dc in each of next 8 dc, *3 dc in next dc, dc in each of next 7 dc, sk next 2 dc, dc in each of next 7 dc; rep from * across to last 10 dc, 3 dc in next dc, dc in each of next 7 dc, sk next dc, dc in 3rd ch of beg 3 skipped chs; ch 2, turn.

Row 3: Dc in next dc, *(PC in next dc, ch 1, skip next dc) 3 times, PC in next dc, 3 dc in next dc, PC in next dc, (ch 1, sk next dc, PC in next dc) 3 times**, sk next 2 dc: rep from * across, ending last rep at **, dec in next 2 dc; ch 2, turn.

Row 4: (Dc in next PC, dc in next ch-1 sp) 3 times, dc in next PC, dc in next dc, *3 dc in next dc, dc in next dc, dc in next PC, (dc in next ch-1 sp, dc in next PC) twice, dc in next ch-1 sp**, sk next 2 PCs, (dc in next ch-1 sp, dc in next PC) 3 times, dc in next dc; rep from * across, ending last rep at **, dec in next 2 sts; ch 2, turn.

Repeat Rows 3 and 4 for pattern. At end of last row, do not ch or turn; finish off.

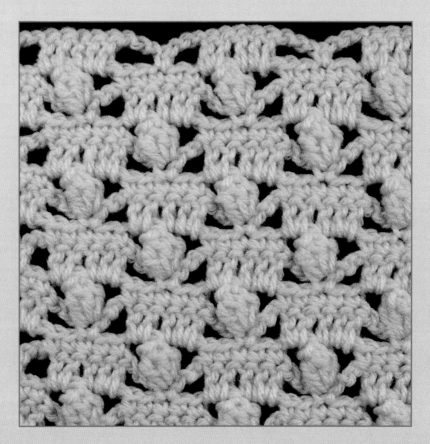

Popcorn Pizzazz

Chain multiple: 10 + 5

STITCH GUIDE

Popcorn (PC): Work 4 dc in specified st; drop lp from hook, insert hook from front to back in top of first dc worked; insert hook in dropped lp and draw through lp on hook: PC made.

Instructions

Row 1 (wrong side): Sc in 2nd ch from hook; *ch 3, skip next 2 chs, dc in each of next 5 chs; ch 3, skip next 2 chs, sc in next ch; rep from * across to last 3 chs, ch 3, skip next next 2 chs, dc in last ch; ch 1, turn.

Row 2 (right side): Sc in first dc; *ch 2, PC in next sc, ch 2, sc in each of next 5 dc; rep from * across, ending last rep with ch 2, dc in last sc; ch 3 (counts as first dc on following row), turn.

Row 3: Work 2 dc in next ch-2 sp; *ch 3, sk next 2 sc, sc in next sc, ch 3, 2 dc in next ch-2 sp, dc in next PC, 2 dc in next ch-2 sp; rep from * across, ending last rep with dc in last sc; ch 1, turn.

Row 4: Sc in each of first 6 dc; *ch 2, PC in next sc, ch 2, sc in each of next 5 dc; rep from * across, ending last rep with ch 2, PC in next dc, ch 2, sc in each of next 2 dc and in 3rd ch of turning ch-3; ch 1, turn.

Row 5: Sc in first sc; *ch 3, 2 dc in next ch-2 sp, dc in next PC, 2 dc in next ch-2 sp, ch 3, sk next 2 sc, sc in next sc; rep from * across, ending last rep with ch 3, dc in last sc; ch 1, turn.

Repeat Rows 2 through 5 for pattern. At end of last row, do not ch or turn; finish off.

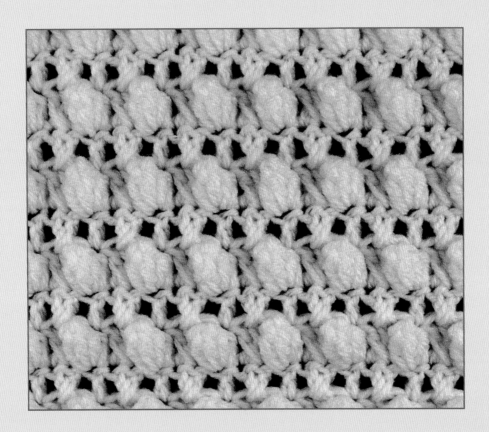

Popcorns Aplenty

Chain multiple: 3

STITCH GUIDE

Popcorn Stitch (PC): Work 5 dc in specified st; drop lp from hook, insert hook from front to back in top of first dc worked, insert hook in dropped lp and draw lp through: PC made.

Instructions

Row 1 (wrong side): Sc in 2nd ch from hook and in each rem ch; ch 3 (counts as first dc on following rows), turn.

Row 2 (right side): Dc in next st; *PC in next st, skip next st, dc in next st, dc in skipped st; rep from * across to last 3 sts, PC in next st, dc in last 2 sts; ch 3, turn.

Row 3: Dc in next dc and in next PC; *skip next dc, dc in next dc, dc in skipped dc, dc in next PC; rep from * across to last 2 sts, dc in each of last 2 sts; ch 3, turn.

Repeat Rows 2 and 3 for pattern. At end of last row, do not ch or turn; finish off.

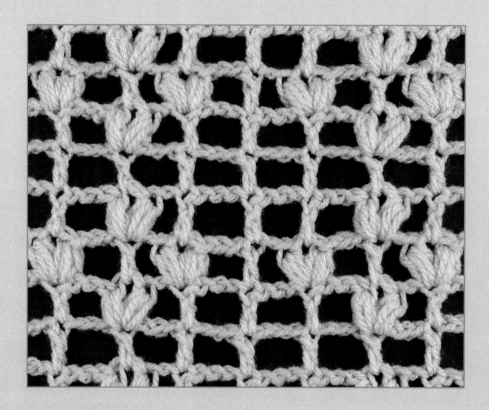

Sweet Puffs

Chain multiple: 16 + 5

STITCH GUIDE

Puff Stitch (PS): *(YO, insert hook into specified st and draw up a lp to height of a dc) 3 times; YO and draw through all 7 lps, ch 1: PS made.

Instructions

Row 1: Dc in 9th ch from hook; *ch 3, skip next 3 chs, dc in next ch; rep from * across, ch 6 (counts as first dc and ch-3 sp on following rows), turn.

Row 2: Dc in next dc; *ch 2, work (PS, ch 1, PS) in next dc; ** ch 2, dc in next dc, (ch 3, dc in next dc) twice; rep from * across, ending last rep at **; ch 2, dc in next dc, ch 3, dc in 6th ch of beg 8 skipped chs; ch 6, turn.

Row 3: *Work (PS, ch 1, PS) in next dc; ch 2, dc in next sp between PS, ch 2, work (PS, ch 1, PS) in next dc, ch 2 **, dc in next dc, ch 2; rep from * across, ending last rep at **; dc in 3rd ch of turning ch; ch 6, turn.

Row 4: Dc in next sp between PS; *ch 2, work (PS, ch 1, PS) in next dc, ch 2, dc in next sp between PS**; ch 3, dc in next dc, ch 3, dc in next sp between PS; rep from * across, ending last rep at **; ch 3, dc in 3rd ch of turning ch; ch 6, turn.

Row 5: Dc in next dc; *ch 3, dc in next sp between PS**, (ch 3, dc in next dc) 3 times; rep from * across, ending last rep at **; ch 3, dc in next dc, dc in 3rd ch of turning ch; ch 6, turn.

Row 6: Dc in next dc; *ch 2, work (PS, ch 1, PS) in next dc**; ch 2, dc in next dc, (ch 3, dc in next dc) twice; rep from * across, ending last rep at **; ch 2, dc in next dc, ch 3, dc in 3rd ch of turning ch; ch 6, turn.

Repeat Rows 3 through 6 for pattern, ending with a Row 5. At end of last row, do not ch or turn; finish off.

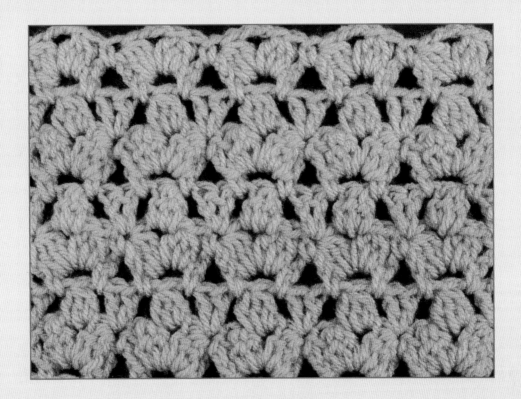

Springtime Bobbles

Chain multiple: 6 + 2

STITCH GUIDE

Bobble (bobble): Keeping last lp of each dc on hook, 3 dc in specified sp; yo, draw through all 4 lps on hook: bobble made.

Instructions

Row 1 (right side): Sc in 8th ch from hook (beg 7 skipped chs count as a ch-2 sp, dc, and 2 skipped chs), ch 3, skip next 2 chs, sc in next ch; *ch 4, sk next 2 chs, sc in next ch, ch 3, sk next 2 chs, sc in next ch; rep from * to last 3 chs, ch 2, sk next 2 chs, dc in last ch; ch 1, turn.

Row 2: Sc in first dc, work (bobble, ch 3, bobble) in next ch-3 sp; *sc in next ch-4 sp, work (bobble, ch 3, bobble) in next ch-3 sp; rep from * to beg 7 skipped chs, sk next 2 skipped chs, sc in next skipped ch; ch 3 (counts as first dc on following rows), turn.

Row 3: Dc in first sc, ch 1, *bobble in next ch-3 sp, ch 1, 2 dc in next sc, ch 1; rep from * to last ch-3 sp; bobble in last ch-3 sp, ch 1, 2 dc in last sc; ch 5 (counts as first dc and ch-2 sp on following rows), turn.

Row 4: Sc in next ch-1 sp, ch 3, *sc in next ch-1 sp, ch 4, sc in next ch-1 sp, ch 3; rep from * to last ch-1 sp; sc in last ch-1 sp, ch 2, dc in 3rd ch of beg ch-3; ch 1, turn.

Row 5: Sc in first dc, work (bobble, ch 3, bobble) in next ch-3 sp; *sc in next ch-4 sp, work (bobble, ch 3, bobble) in next ch-3 sp; rep from * to turning ch-5; sc in 3rd ch of turning ch-5; ch 3, turn.

Repeat Rows 3 through 5 for pattern. At end of last row, do not ch or turn; finish off.

Field of Clusters

Chain multiple: 5 + 2

STITCH GUIDE

Cluster (Cl): (YO, insert hook in next ch and draw up a lp, YO and draw through 2 lps) 4 times; YO and draw through all 5 lps on hook: Cl made in 4th ch in first row. On following rows work Cl in 3-ch sp.

Instructions

Row 1 (wrong side): Sc in 2nd ch from hook; *ch 3, Cl over next 4 chs; ch 1, sc in next ch; rep from * across; ch 5, turn.

Row 2 (right side): Sc in next Cl; *ch 3, Cl in next ch-3 sp, ch 1, sc in next Cl; rep from * across, ending last rep with ch 3, Cl in next ch-3 sp, ch 1, dc in last sc; ch 1, turn.

Row 3: Skip first st, sc in next Cl; *ch 3, Cl in next ch-3 sp, ch 1, sc in next Cl; rep from * across, ending last rep with sc in sp formed by turning ch; ch 5, turn.

Repeat Rows 2 and 3 for pattern. At end of last row, do not ch or turn; finish off.

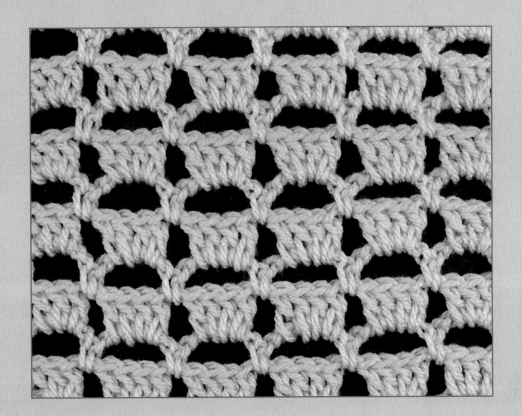

Look-a-Like Clusters

Chain multiple: 5 + 1

Instructions

Row 1 (right side): Dc in 4th ch from hook (beg ch-3 counts as a dc) and in each of next 2 chs; *ch 1, sk next ch, dc in each of next 4 chs; rep from * across; ch 1, turn.

Row 2: Sc in first dc; *ch 5, sc in next ch-1 sp; rep from * across, ending last rep with ch 5, sc in top of turning ch; ch 3 (counts as first dc on following row), turn.

Row 3: 3 dc in first ch-5 sp; *ch 1, 4 dc in next ch-5 sp; rep from * to last ch-5 sp, ch 1, 3 dc in last ch-5 sp, dc in last sc; ch 1, turn.

Repeat Rows 2 and 3 for pattern. At end of last row, do not ch or turn; finish off.

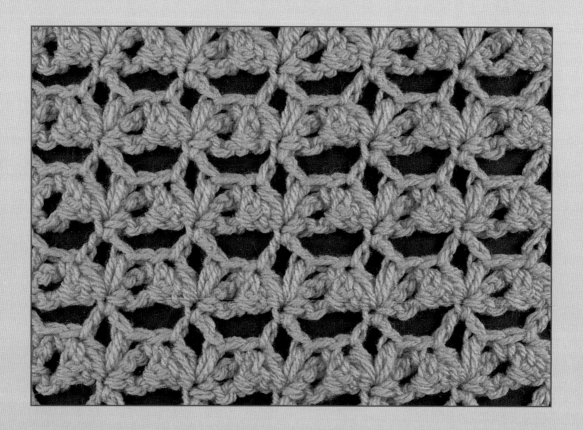

Bobble Delight

Chain multiple: 4 + 2

STITCH GUIDE

Bobble (BB): *YO, insert hook in specified st and draw up a lp to height of dc; rep from * once more in same st or sp; YO and draw through all 5 lps on hook: BB made.

Yst: Tr in specified st, ch 1, dc in center of post (vertical bar) of tr just made: Yst made.

Instructions

Row 1 (wrong side): Sc in 2nd ch from hook; *ch 4, work Yst in top of last sc made, skip next 3 chs, sc in next ch; rep from * across; ch 6, turn.

Row 2 (right side): BB in first sc, sc in next ch-4 sp; *work (BB, ch 3, BB) in next sc, sc in next ch-4 sp; rep from * across to last sc; work (BB, ch 1, tr) in last sc; ch 1, turn.

Row 3: Sc in first tr; *ch 4, work Yst in top of last sc made, sc in next ch-3 sp; rep from * across, working last sc in turning ch-6 sp; ch 6, turn.

Repeat Rows 2 and 3 for pattern. At end of last row, do not ch or turn; finish off.

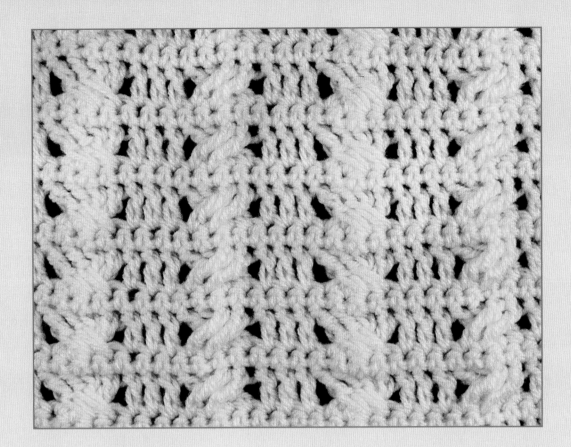

Turns and Twists

Chain multiple: 7 + 4

Instructions

Row 1 (wrong side): Sc in 2nd ch from hook and in each rem ch; ch 3 (counts as first dc on following rows), turn.

Row 2 (right side): Dc in each of next 2 sts; *skip next 2 sts, tr in each of next 2 sts; working behind 2 tr just made, tr in first skipped st, then tr in next skipped st; dc in each of next 3 sts; skip next 2 sts, tr in next 2 sts; working in front of 2 tr just made, tr in first skipped st, tr in next skipped st; dc in each of next 3 sts; rep from * across; ch 1, turn.

Row 3: Sc in each st across, ch 3, turn.

Repeat Rows 2 and 3 for pattern. At end of last row, do not ch or turn; finish off.

Double Delights

Chain multiple: 12 + 4

STITCH GUIDE

Front Popcorn (FPC): Work 4 dc in specified st or sp; drop lp from hook, insert hook from front to back through top of first dc made, insert hook in dropped lp and draw it through lp on hook: FPC made.

Back Popcorn (BPC): Work 4 dc in specified ch or sp; drop lp from hook, insert hook from back to front through top of first dc made, insert hook in dropped lp and draw it through lp on hook: BPC made.

Front Popcorn shell (FPC shell): Work (FPC, ch 3, FPC) in specified st or sp: FPC shell made.

Back Popcorn shell (BPC shell): Work (BPC, ch 3, BPC) in specified st or sp: BPC shell made.

Instructions

Row 1 (right side): In 5th ch from hook work FPC; *ch 3, skip next 4 chs, sc in next ch; ch 3, skip next ch, sc in next ch; ch 3**, skip next 4 chs, FPC shell in next ch; rep from * across, ending last rep at **; (FPc, ch 1, dc) in last ch; ch 3, turn.

Row 2: Sc in next ch-1 sp; *ch 3, skip next ch-3 sp, work BPC shell in next ch-3 sp, ch 3**; (sc, ch 3, sc) in center ch-3 sp of shell; rep from * across, ending last rep at **; sc in turning ch sp, ch 1, hdc in 3rd ch of turning ch; ch 4, turn.

Row 3: Work FPC in next ch-1 sp; *ch 3, (sc, ch 3, sc) in ch-3 sp of next shell, ch 3**, skip next ch-3 sp, work FPC shell in next ch-3 sp; rep from * across, ending last rep at **; work (FPC, ch 1, dc) in turning ch sp; ch 3, turn.

Repeat Rows 2 and 3 for pattern. At end of last row, do not ch or turn; finish off.

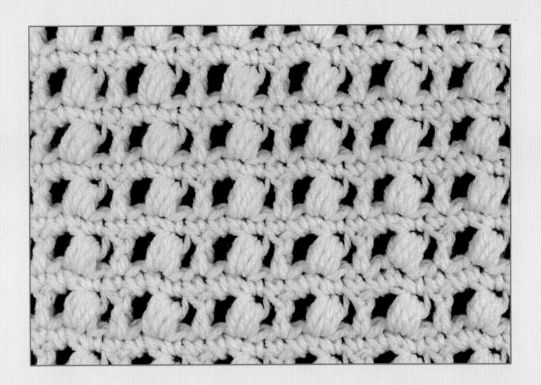

Mini Puffs

Chain multiple: 4

STITCH GUIDE

Puff Stitch (PS): (YO, insert hook in specified st and draw up a lp to height of a dc) 4 times: YO and draw through all 9 lps on hook: PS made.

Instructions

Row 1: Sc in 2nd ch from hook and in each rem ch; ch 3 (counts as first dc on following row), turn.

Row 2: *Dc in next st, ch 1, skip next st, PS in next st, ch 1, skip next st; rep from * across to last 2 sts, dc in each of last 2 sts; ch 1, turn.

Row 3: Sc in each st and in each ch-1 sp across; ch 3, turn.

Repeat Rows 2 and 3 for pattern. At end of last row, do not ch or turn; finish off.

Popcorn Duet

Chain multiple: 4 + 2

Two colors: color A and color B

STITCH GUIDE

Popcorn (PC): Work 5 dc in specified st. Drop lp from hook, insert hook from front to back in top of first dc made, hook dropped lp and draw through: PC made.

Instructions

Work starting ch with color A.

Row 1 (wrong side): With color A, sc in 2nd ch from hook and in each rem ch; ch 4 (counts as first dc and ch-1 sp on following row), turn.

Row 2 (right side): Sk next sc; *PC in next sc, ch 1, sk next sc, dc in next sc, ch 1, sk next sc; rep from * across to last sc; dc in last sc, changing to color B in last st; ch 1, turn.

Row 3: With color B, sc in each st and in each ch-1 sp across, ending with sc in turning ch sp and sc in 3rd ch of turning ch; ch 4, turn.

Row 4: With color B, rep Row 2, changing to color A in last st; ch 1, turn.

Repeat Rows 3 and 4 for pattern, alternating two rows of each color. At end of last row, do not ch or turn; finish off.

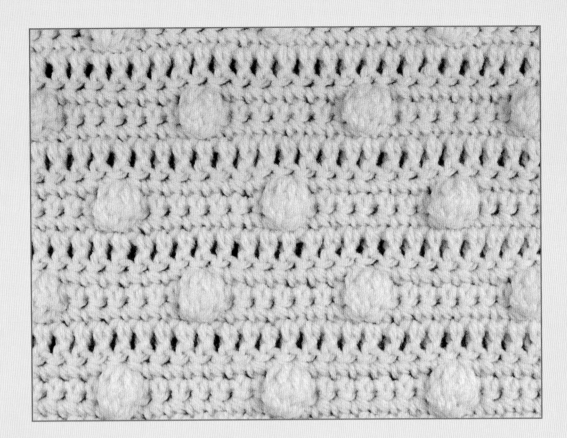

Puff Drops

Chain multiple: 8 + 3

STITCH GUIDE

Puff Stitch (PS): (YO, insert hook in specified st and draw up a lp to height of a dc, YO and draw through 2 lps) 4 times; YO and draw through 5 lps, ch 1: PS made.

Instructions

Row 1 (right side): Dc in 4th ch from hook (beg 3 skipped chs count as a dc) and in each rem ch; ch 1, turn.

Row 2: Sc in each st across to beg 3 skipped chs; sc in 3rd ch of beg 3 skipped chs; ch 1, turn.

Row 3: Sc in each of first 8 sc, PS in next sc; *sc in next 7 sc, PS in next sc; rep from * across, ending last rep with sc in last 8 sc; ch 1, turn.

Row 4: Sc in each sc and in each PS, skipping ch-1 sp of each PS; ch 3 (counts as first dc on following row), turn.

Row 5: Dc in each st across, ch 1, turn.

Row 6: Sc in each st across to turning ch-3; sc in 3rd ch of turning ch-3; ch 1, turn.

Row 7: Sc in each of first 4 sc, PS in next sc; *sc in each of next 7 sc, PS in next sc; rep from * across, ending last rep with sc in each of last 4 sc; ch 1, turn.

Row 8: Sc in each sc and in each PS, skipping ch-1 sp of each PS; ch 3, turn.

Row 9: Rep Row 5.

Repeat Rows 2 through 9 for pattern. At end of last row, do not ch or turn; finish off.

Puff Posies

Chain multiple: 6 + 2

STITCH GUIDE

V-Stitch (V-St): In specified st work (dc, ch 2, dc): V-St made.

Puff Stitch (PS): (YO, insert hook in specified sp and draw up a lp to height of a dc) 3 times, in same lp, YO and draw through 7 lps: PS made.

Puff Stitch Shell (PS shell): In specified sp work (PS, ch 2) twice, PS in same sp: PS shell made.

Instructions

Row 1: Dc in 4th ch from hook (beg 3 skipped chs count as a dc) and in each rem ch; ch 1, turn.

Row 2: Sc in first dc; *ch 2, skip next 2 dc, V-St in next dc, ch 2, skip next 2 dc, sc in next dc; rep from * across, ending last rep with sc in top of turning ch; ch 4 (counts as first dc and ch-1 sp on following row), turn.

Row 3: *Work PS shell in ch-2 sp of next V-St, ch 1; rep from * across to last V-St, work PS shell in last V-St, tr in last sc; ch 4, turn.

Row 4: *Dc in next ch-2 sp, ch 1, dc in next ch-2 sp, ch 1, dc in next ch-1 sp, ch 1; rep from * across, ending last rep with dc in 3rd ch of turning ch-4; ch 3, turn.

Row 5: Dc in each ch-1 sp and in each dc across, ending last rep with dc in turning ch sp, dc in 3rd ch of turning ch; ch 1, turn.

Repeat Rows 2 through 5 for pattern. At end of last row, do not ch or turn; finish off.

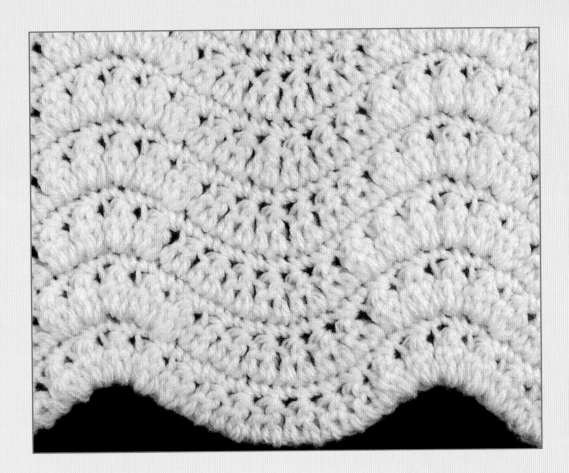

Wavy Bobbles

Chain multiple: 17 + 2

STITCH GUIDE

Bobble (bobble): Keeping last lp of each dc on hook, 3 dc in specified st; yo, draw through all 4 lps on hook: bobble made.

Decrease (dec): (YO and draw up a lp in next st, YO and draw through first 2 lps on hook) twice, YO and draw through remaining 3 lps on hook: 1 dec made.

Instructions

Row 1: Dc in 4th ch from hook (beg 3 skipped chs count as a dc); dec twice; *ch 1, (bobble, in next ch, ch 1) 5 times **, dec 6 times; rep from * across, ending last rep at **; dec 3 times; ch 1, turn.

Row 2: Sc in each st and in each ch-1 sp across, ch 3 (counts as first dc on following rows), turn.

Row 3: Dc in next sc, dec twice; *ch 1, (bobble, in next ch, ch 1) 5 times **, dec 6 times; rep from * across, ending last rep at **; dec 3 times; ch 1, turn.

Row 4: Sc in each st and in each ch-1 sp across; ch 3, turn.

Repeat Rows 3 and 4 for pattern. At end of last row, do not ch or turn; finish off.

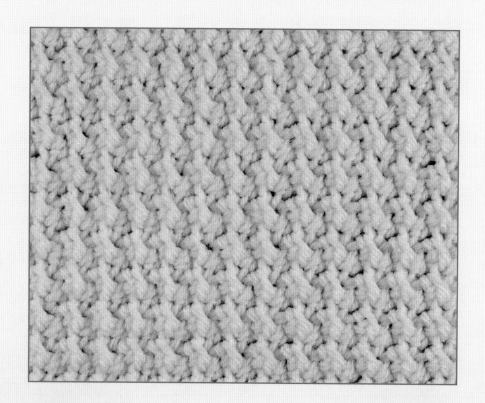

Mini Bobbles

Chain multiple: 2 + 1

Instructions

Note: *Work all sl sts loosely.*

Row 1: Sl st in 3rd ch from hook (beg 2 skipped chs count as an hdc); *hdc in next ch, sl st in next ch; rep from * across; ch 2 (counts as first hdc on following row), turn.

Row 2 (right side): Skip first sl st; *sl st in next hdc, hdc in next sl st; rep from * across; sl st in 2nd ch of beg 2 skipped chs; ch 2, turn.

Row 3: Skip first sl st; *sl st in next hdc, hdc in next sl st; rep from * across; sl st in 2nd ch of turning ch-2; ch 2, turn.

Repeat Row 3 for pattern. At end of last row, do not ch or turn; finish off.

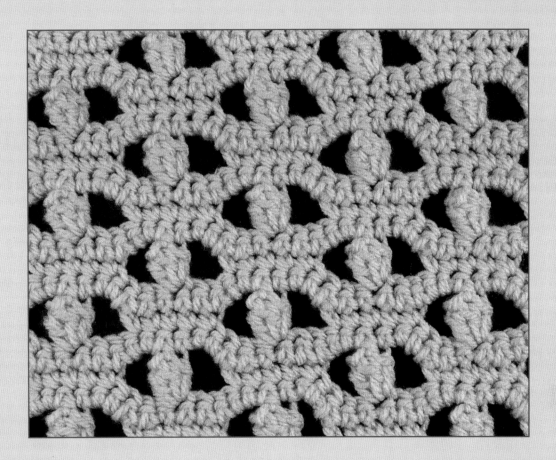

In-Between Pops

Chain multiple: 10 + 2

STITCH GUIDE

Popcorn (PC): Work 4 dc in same st; drop lp from hook, insert hook from front to back in top of first dc made; pick up dropped lp and draw through lp on hook: PC made.

Instructions

Row 1: Sc in 2nd ch from hook and in each rem ch; ch 1, turn.

Row 2 (right side): Sc in each of first 3 sc; *ch 3, skip next 2 sc, PC in next sc, ch 3, skip next 2 sc, sc in each of next 5 sc; rep from * across, ending last rep with sc in each of last 3 sc; ch 1, turn.

Row 3: Sc in each of first 3 sc; *3 sc in ch-3 sp, sc in PC, 3 sc in ch-3 sp, sc in each of next 5 sc; rep from * across, ending last rep with sc in each of last 3 sc; ch 6, turn.

Row 4: Skip first 4 sc; *sc in each of next 5 sc**, ch 3, skip next 3 sc, PC in next sc, ch 3, skip next 3 sc; rep from * across, ending last rep at **; ch 3, dc in last sc; ch 1, turn.

Row 5: Sc in first dc, 3 sc in next ch-3 sp; *sc in each of next 5 sc, 3 sc in next ch-3 sp, sc in next PC, 3 sc in next ch-3 sp; rep from * across, ending last rep with 3 sc in turning ch lp, sc in 3rd ch of turning ch; ch 1, turn.

Row 6: Sc in each of first 3 sc; *ch 3, skip next 3 sc, PC in next sc; ch 3, skip next 3 sc, sc in each of next 5 sc; rep from * across, ending last rep with sc in each of last 3 sc; ch 1, turn.

Repeat Rows 3 through 6 for pattern. At end of last row, do not ch or turn; finish off.

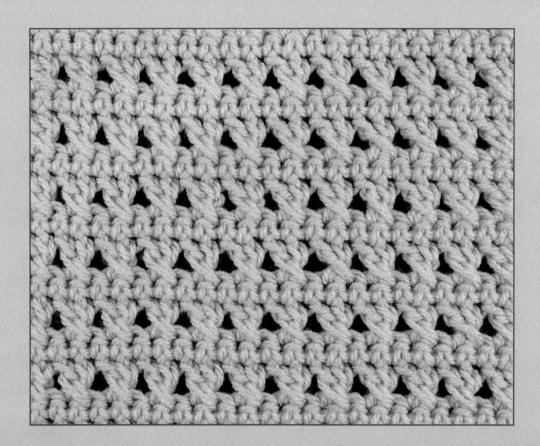

Criss Cross

Chain multiple: Any uneven number

Instructions

Row 1 (wrong side): Sc in 2nd ch from hook and in each rem ch; ch 3 (counts as first dc on following rows), turn.

Row 2 (right side): * Sk next sc, dc in next sc, dc in skipped sc; rep from * across to last st; dc in last st; ch 1, turn.

Row 3: Sc in each dc across; ch 3, turn.

Repeat Rows 2 and 3 for pattern, ending with a Row 2. At end of last row, do not ch or turn; finish off.

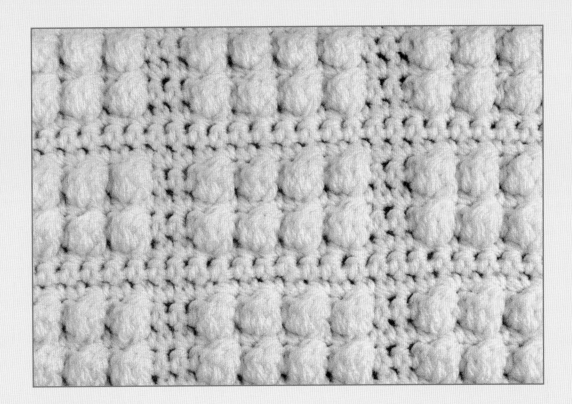

Boxes of Clusters

Chain multiple: 10 + 4

STITCH GUIDE

Cluster (Cl): (YO, insert hook in specified st and draw up a $1/2$" lp ; YO and draw through 2 lps on hook) 3 times; YO and draw through all 4 lps on hook: Cl made.

Instructions

Row 1 (right side): Sc in 2nd ch from hook and in each rem ch; ch 1, turn.

Rows 2 and 3: Sc in each sc; ch 1, turn.

Row 4: Sc in each of first 3 sc; *(Cl in next st, sc in next st) 3 times; Cl in next st; sc in each of next 3 sc; rep from * across; ch 1, turn.

Row 5: Sc in each sc and in each Cl across; ch 1, turn.

Row 6: Rep Row 4.

Row 7: Sc in each sc and in each Cl across; ch 1, turn.

Rows 8 and 9: Sc in each sc across; ch 1, turn.

Repeat Rows 4 through 9 for pattern. At end of last row, do not ch or turn; finish off.

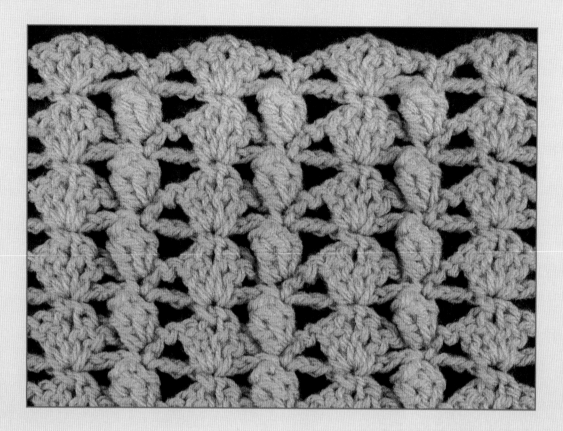

Treasures

Chain multiple: 8 + 2

STITCH GUIDE

Shell: Work (2 dc, ch 1, 2 dc) all in same st: shell made.

Popcorn (PC): Work 4 dc in same st; drop lp from hook, insert hook from front to back in top of first dc made, pick up dropped lp and draw through: PC made.

Instructions

Row 1: Sc in 2nd ch from hook; *ch 2, skip next 3 chs, shell in next ch; ch 2, skip next 3 chs, sc in next ch; rep from * across; ch 3 (counts as first dc on following rows), turn.

Row 2 (right side): Dc in first sc; *ch 3, sc in center ch-1 sp of next shell, ch 3**, work PC in next sc; rep from * across, ending last rep at **; dc in last sc, ch 1, turn.

Row 3: Sc in first dc; *ch 2, shell in next sc; ch 2, sc in next PC; rep from * across, ending last rep with shell in last sc; ch 2, sc in last dc; do not work in turning ch; ch 3, turn.

Repeat Rows 2 and 3 for pattern. At end of last row, do not ch or turn; finish off.

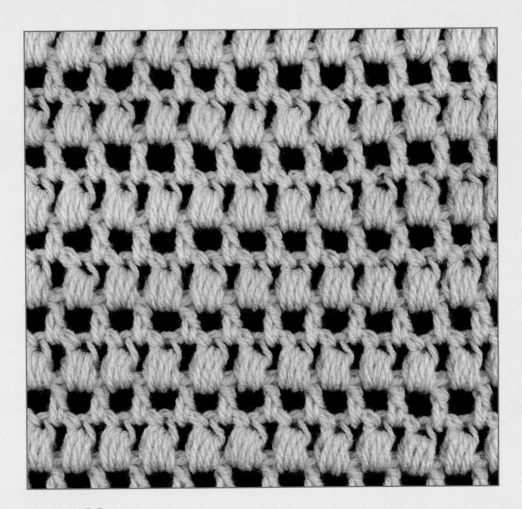

Dream Puffs

Chain multiple: Any even number

STITCH GUIDE

Puff stitch (PS): (YO, insert hook in specified sp and draw up a lp to height of a dc) 4 times; YO and draw through all 9 lps: PS made.

Instructions

Row 1: Sc in 2nd ch from hook and in each rem ch; ch 4 (counts as first dc and ch-1 sp on following rows), turn.

Row 2: Skip next sc, dc in next dc; *ch 1, skip next sc, dc in next sc; rep from * across; ch 4, turn.

Row 3: *PS in next ch-1 sp, ch 2; rep from * across to turning ch sp, PS in turning ch sp, ch 1, dc in 3rd ch of turning ch-4; ch 4, turn.

Row 4: *Dc in next ch-2 sp, ch 1; rep from * across, ending last rep with dc in last ch-2 sp, ch 1, dc in 3rd ch of turning ch-4; ch 4, turn.

Repeat Rows 3 and 4 for pattern. At end of last row, do not ch or turn; finish off.

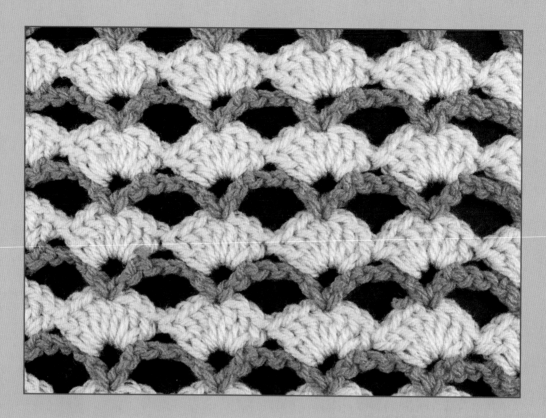

Shells by the Sea

Chain multiple: 6 + 4

Two colors: color A and color B

STITCH GUIDE

V-Stitch (V-St): Work (dc, ch 2, dc) all in same st: V-St made.

Shell: Work 7 dc all in same st: shell made.

Instructions

Note: *Work starting chain with color A.*

Row 1 (wrong side): With color A, dc in 5th ch from hook; *ch 2, sk next 5 chs, V-St in next ch; rep from * across to last 5 chs, sk next 4 chs, work (dc, ch 1, dc) in last ch, changing to color B in last dc; with color B, ch 3 (counts as first dc on following row), turn.

Row 2 (right side): With color B, 3 dc in first ch-1 sp; *work shell in ch-2 sp of next V-St; rep from * across, ending last rep with 4 dc in turning ch sp, changing to color A in last dc; with color A, ch 4 (counts as first dc and ch-1 sp on following row), turn.

Row 3: With color A, dc in base of ch; *ch 2, V-St in center dc of next shell; rep from * across, ending last rep with ch 2, (dc, ch 1, dc) in 3rd ch of turning ch-4, changing to color B in last dc; with color B, ch 3, turn.

Repeat Rows 2 and 3 for pattern. At end of last row, do not ch or turn; finish off.

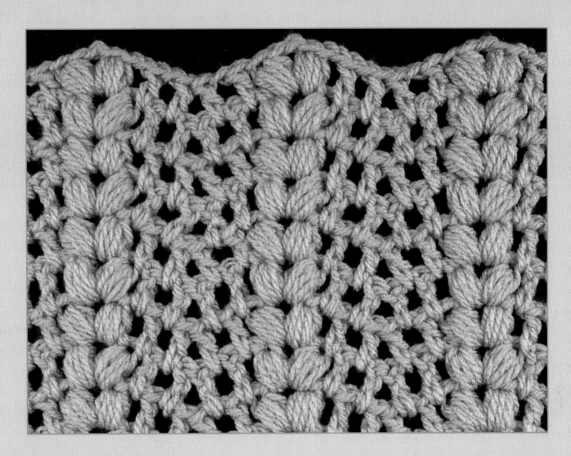

Lace and Puffs

Chain multiple: 12 + 4

STITCH GUIDE

Puff stitch (PS): (YO, insert hook in specified ch or st and draw up a lp to height of a dc) 4 times, YO and draw through all 9 lps on hook: PS made.

Instructions

Row 1: Dc in 6th ch from hook; ch 1, skip next ch, dc in next ch, ch 1, skip next ch, work (PS, ch 2, PS) in next ch; *(ch 1, skip next ch, dc in next ch) twice; skip next 3 chs, (dc in next ch, ch 1, skip next ch) twice, work (PS, ch 2, PS) in next ch; rep from * across to last 7 chs; (ch 1, skip next ch, dc in next ch) twice; skip next ch, dc in last ch; ch 3 (counts as first dc on following row), turn.

Row 2: *(Dc in next ch-1 sp, ch 1) twice; work (PS, ch 2, PS) in next ch-2 sp; (ch 1, dc in next ch-1 sp) twice; rep from * across, ending last rep with dc in top of turning ch; ch 3, turn.

Repeat Row 2 for pattern. At end of last row, do not ch or turn; finish off.

Popcorn Paths

Chain multiple: 8 + 2

STITCH GUIDE

Popcorn (PC): 3 hdc in specified st; remove hook from lp, insert hook from front to back in top of first hdc made, insert hook into dropped lp and draw through: PC made.

Instructions

Row 1 (wrong side): Sc in 2nd ch from hook and in each rem ch; ch 2 (counts as first hdc on following rows), turn.

Row 2 (right side): Hdc in each of next 2 sc; *ch 1, skip next sc, PC in next sc, ch 1, skip next sc, hdc in each of next 5 sc; rep from * across, ending last rep with hdc in last 3 sc; ch 2, turn.

Row 3: Hdc in each of next 2 hdc; *PC in next ch-1 sp, ch 1, skip next PC, PC in next ch-1 sp, hdc in each of next 5 hdc; rep from * across, ending last rep with hdc in last 2 hdc and in 2nd ch of turning ch-2; ch 2, turn.

Row 4: Hdc in each of next 2 hdc; *ch 1, skip next PC, PC in next ch-1 sp, ch 1, skip next PC, hdc in each of next 5 hdc; rep from * across, ending last rep with hdc in last 2 hdc and in 2nd ch of turning ch-2; ch 2, turn.

Repeat Rows 3 and 4 for pattern. At end of last row, do not ch or turn; finish off.

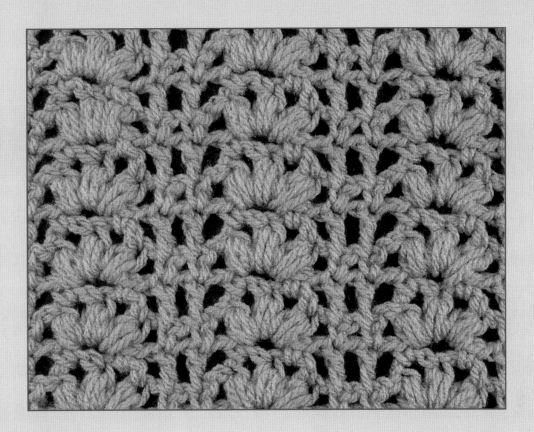

Puff Trellis

Chain multiple: 9 + 2

STITCH GUIDE

Puff Stitch (PS): (YO, insert hook in specified sp, YO and draw up a lp to height of a dc) 3 times, YO and draw through all 7 lps on hook: PS made.

Instructions

Row 1 (right side): Sc in 2nd ch from hook and in next ch, ch 1, skip next ch, sc in next ch, ch 3, skip next 2 chs, sc in next ch; *(ch 1, skip next ch, sc in next ch) 3 times; ch 3, skip next 2 chs, sc in next ch; rep from * to last 3 chs, ch 1, skip next ch, sc in each of last 2 chs; ch 1, turn.

Row 2: Sc in each of first 2 sc, ch 1, work (PS, ch 3) twice in next ch-3 sp; PS in same sp; ch 2, skip next sc, sc in next sc; *ch 1, sc in next sc, ch 1, work (PS, ch 3) twice in next ch-3 sp; PS in same sp; ch 2, skip next sc, sc in next sc; rep from * to last sc; sc in last sc; ch 3 (counts as first dc on following rows), turn.

Row 3: Dc in next sc, ch 1, sc in next ch-3 sp, ch 3, sc in next ch-3 sp; *ch 1, (dc in next sc, ch 1) twice, sc in next ch-3 sp, ch 3, sc in next ch-3 sp; rep from * to last 2 sc, ch 1, dc in each of last 2 sc; ch 1, turn.

Row 4: Sc in each of first 2 dc, ch 1, work (PS, ch 3) twice in next ch-3 sp; PS in same sp; ch 2; *(sc in next dc, ch 1) twice, work (PS, ch 3) twice in next ch-3 sp; PS in same sp; ch 2; rep from * to last 2 dc, sc in each of last 2 dc; ch 3, turn.

Repeat Rows 3 and 4 for pattern; ending with a Row 3. At end of last row, do not ch or turn; finish off.

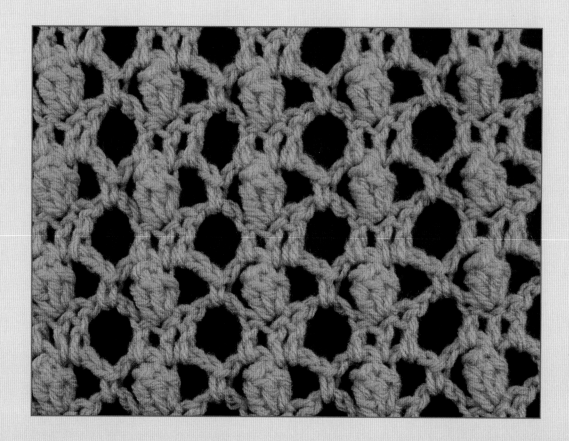

Popcorns in the Air

Chain multiple: 6 + 1

STITCH GUIDE

Popcorn (PC): Work 4 dc in specified st; drop lp from hook, insert hook from front to back in first dc; pick up dropped lp and draw through lp on hook: PC made.

Instructions

Row 1 (right side): Sc in 10th ch from hook; *ch 3, skip next 2 chs, PC in next ch, ch 3, skip next 2 chs, sc in next ch; rep from * to last 3 chs; ch 3, skip next 2 chs, dc in last ch; ch 3 (counts as first dc on following row), turn.

Row 2: Dc in next ch-3 sp; *ch 3, dc in next ch-3 sp, dc in next PC, dc in next ch-3 sp; rep from * across, ending last rep with ch 3, 2 dc in turning ch sp; ch 6, turn.

Row 3: Sc in next ch-3 sp; *ch 3, sk next dc, PC in next dc, ch 3, sc in next ch-3 sp; rep from * across, ending last rep with ch 3, dc in top of turning ch; ch 3, turn.

Repeat Rows 2 and 3 for pattern, ending with a Row 2. At end of last row, do not ch or turn; finish off.

Open Baskets

Chain multiple: 3

STITCH GUIDE

Basket Stitch (BS): Working horizontally around post (vertical bar) of specified dc work (sc, hdc, 2 dc, tr): BS made.

Instructions

Row 1 (right side): Sc in 2nd ch from hook and in each rem ch; ch 3 (counts as first dc on following row), turn.

Row 2: Dc in each sc; ch 1, turn.

Row 3: BS around next dc, skip next 2 dc, sc in next dc; *BS around dc in which sc was just worked, skip next 2 dc, sc in next dc; rep from * across; ch 3, turn.

Row 4: Dc in each st behind each BS; ch 1, turn.

Row 5: BS around next dc, skip next 2 dc, sc in next dc; *BS around dc in which sc was just worked, skip next 2 dc, sc in next dc; rep from * across; ch 1, turn.

Row 6: Sc in each st behind each BS; ch 1, turn.

Row 7: Sc in each sc; ch 3, turn.

Repeat Rows 2 through 7 for pattern. At end of last row, do not ch or turn; finish off.

Popcorn Fascination

Chain multiple: 15 + 14

STITCH GUIDE

Popcorn (PC): Work 5 dc in specified st; drop lp from hook, insert hook from front to back to front in top of first dc made, pick up dropped lp and draw lp through; ch 1: PC made.

Instructions

Row 1 (wrong side): Dc in 5th ch from hook and in next ch; *skip next 2 chs, dc in next ch, skip next 2 chs, dc in each of next 2 chs, ch 2**; dc in each of next 7 chs, ch 2, 2 dc in next ch; rep from * across, ending last rep at **; dc in last ch; ch 5, turn.

Row 2 (right side): 2 dc in next ch-2 sp; *skip next 2 dc, dc in next dc, skip next 2 dc**, 2 dc in next ch-2 sp; ch 2, dc in each of next 2 dc, ch 1, skip next dc, PC in next dc, ch 1, skip next dc, dc in each of next 2 dc, ch 2, 2 dc in next ch-2 sp; rep from * across, ending last rep at **; 2 dc in end sp, ch 2, dc in 3rd ch of turning ch; ch 5, turn.

Row 3: 2 dc in next ch-2 sp; *skip next 2 dc, dc in next dc**, 2 dc in next ch-2 sp; ch 2; dc in each of next 2 dc, dc in next ch-1 sp, dc in next PC, dc in next ch-1 sp, dc in each of next 2 dc, ch 2, 2 dc in next ch-2 sp, rep from * across, ending last rep at**; 2 dc in end sp, dc in 3rd ch of turning ch; ch 5, turn.

Repeat Rows 2 and 3 for pattern. At end of last row, do not ch or turn; finish off.

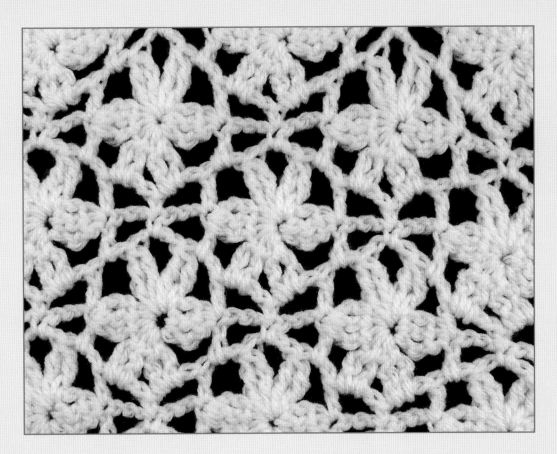

Floral Circles

Chain multiple: 12 + 10

STITCH GUIDE

Bobble (BB): *YO twice, insert hook in specified st or sp and draw up a lp, (YO and draw through 2 lps on hook) twice; rep from * once in same st or sp; YO and draw through all 3 lps on hook: BB made.

Shell: Work (BB, ch 3, BB) in specified ch or st: shell made.

Bobble cluster (BBcl): *YO twice, insert hook in top of last dc (or in 3rd ch of turning ch-6) and draw up a lp, (YO and draw through 2 lps on hook) twice; rep from * once in top of same dc (or in same ch); **YO twice, insert hook in next ch sp and draw up a lp, (YO and draw through 2 lps on hook) twice; rep from ** once in same ch sp***; rep from ** to *** once in next ch sp; YO and draw through all 7 lps on hook, ch 1: BBcl made.

Instructions

Row 1: Shell in 7th ch from hook; *ch 2, skip next 2 chs, dc in next ch, ch 3, skip next 2 chs, sc in next ch, ch 3, skip next 2 chs, dc in next ch, ch 2, skip next 2 chs, shell in next ch; rep from * across to last 3 chs; skip next 2 chs, dc in last ch; ch 6 (counts as first dc and ch-3 sp on following rows), turn.

Row 2: Sc in next ch-3 sp, ch 3, begin flower with ch 3, work BBcl, ch 3, BB in top of last BBcl (4 petals completed), dc in next ch sp, ch 3; rep from * across, ending sc in next ch-3 sp, ch 3, sc in 3rd ch of beg ch-6. Ch 6, turn.

Row 3: *Sc in next st, ch 3, dc in next dc, ch 2, shell in top of next BBcl (flower completed), ch 2, dc in next dc, ch 3; rep from * across, ending sc in next st, ch 3, dc in 3rd ch of turning ch-6; ch 6, turn.

Row 4: *BBcl, ch 3, BB in top of last BBcl; dc in next ch-2 sp, ch 3, sc in next ch-3 sp, ch 3, dc in next ch-2 sp, ch 3; rep from * across to last ch-3 sp and turning ch-3, work BBcl, ch 3, BB in top of last BBcl, dc in 3rd ch of turning ch-6; ch 3 (counts as first dc on next rows), turn.

Row 5: *Shell in top of next BBcl**; ch 2, dc in next dc, ch 3, sc in next sc, ch 3, dc in next dc, ch 2; rep from * across, ending last rep at **; dc in 3rd ch of turning ch-6; ch 6, turn.

Repeat Rows 2 through 5 for pattern. At end of last row, do not ch or turn; finish off.

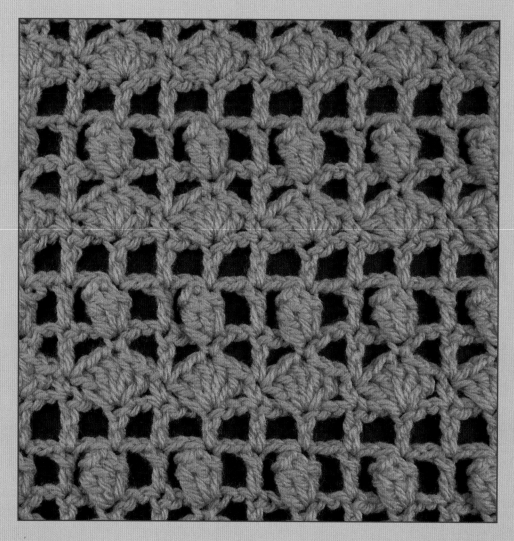

Easy Shells and Popcorns

Chain multiple: 6

STITCH GUIDE

Popcorn (PC): Work 4 dc all in same st; drop lp from hook, insert hook from front to back in top of first dc made, insert hook in dropped lp and draw through: PC made.

Shell: Work 5 dc all in same st: shell made.

Instructions

Row 1 (right side): Work PC in 9th ch from hook; *ch 2, skip next 2 chs, dc in next ch, ch 2, skip next 2 chs, PC in next ch; rep from * across ending ch 2, skip 2 chs, dc in last ch; ch 5 (counts as first dc and ch-2 sp on following row), turn.

Row 2: Dc in next PC; *ch 2, dc in next dc, ch 2 **; dc in next PC, ch 2; rep from * across, ending last rep at **; skip next 2 chs of turning ch, dc in next ch; ch 1, turn.

Row 3: Sc in first dc; *shell in next dc, sc in next dc; rep from * across, ending last rep with sc in 3rd ch of turning ch; ch 5, turn.

Row 4: Sc in 3rd dc of next shell, ch 2, dc in next sc; *ch 2, sc in 3rd dc of next shell, ch 2, dc in next sc; rep from * across; ch 5, turn.

Row 5: Work PC in next sc, ch 2, dc in next dc; *ch 2, PC in next sc, ch 2, dc in next dc; rep from * across, ending last rep with dc in 3rd ch of turning ch; ch 5, turn.

Repeat Rows 2 through 5 for pattern. At end of last row, do not ch or turn; finish off.

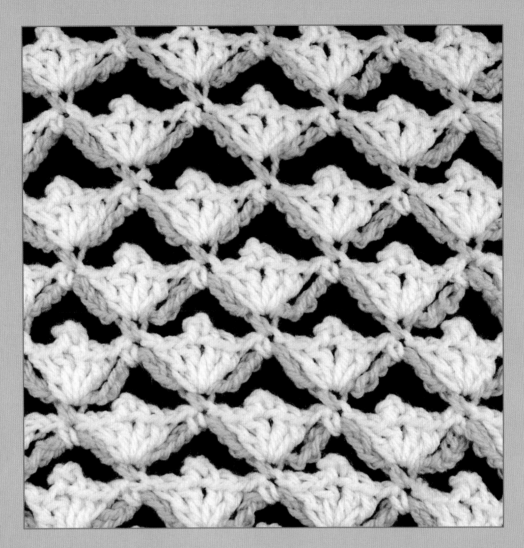

Picot Shells

Chain multiple: 6 + 2

Two colors: color A and color B.

STITCH GUIDE

Picot: Ch 3, sl st in base of ch: picot made.

Shell: In specified st work (2 dc, picot, 2 dc): shell made.

Instructions

Note: *Work starting chain with color A. All rows are worked on the right side; finish off at the end of each row, do not turn. With right side facing you, join new color yarn in first st at right.*

Row 1: With color A, sc in 2nd ch from hook; *ch 9, skip next 5 chs, sc in next ch; rep from * across; finish off color A.

Row 2: Join color B in first sc at right with sl st; ch 4, 2 dc in base of ch; *ch 1, sc in next ch-9 sp, ch 1**; shell in next sc; rep from * across, ending last rep at **; 3 dc in last sc, finish off color B.

Row 3: Join color A in top of turning ch at right; ch 8 (counts as a tr and ch-4 sp), sc in next sc; *ch 9, sc in next sc; rep from * across, ending last rep with ch 4, tr in last dc; finish off color A.

Row 4: Join color B with sc in 4th ch of turning ch, ch 1; *shell in next sc; ch 1, sc in next ch-9 sp, ch 1; rep from * across, ending last rep with sc in last tr; finish off color B.

Row 5: Join color A with sc in first sc at right; *ch 9, sc in next sc; rep from * across; finish off color A.

Repeat Rows 2 through 5 for pattern. At end of last row, do not ch or turn; finish off.

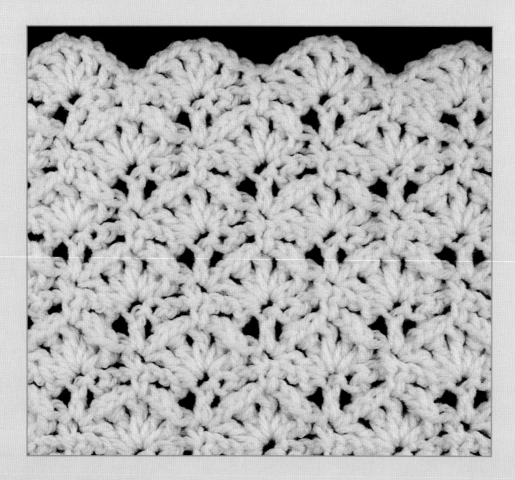

Romantic Fans

Chain multiple: 8 + 2

STITCH GUIDE

Fan: Work (dc, ch 1) 4 times in specified st, dc in same st: Fan made.

Back post double crochet (BPdc): YO, insert hook from back to front to back around post (vertical bar) of specified st; YO and draw up a lp to height of a dc; (YO and draw through 2 lps) twice: BPdc made.

Instructions

Row 1 (right side): Sc in 2nd ch from hook; *sk next 3 chs, work fan in next ch**; sk next 3 chs, sc in next ch; rep from * across, ending last rep at **; sk next 3 chs, sc in last ch; ch 3 (counts as first dc on following row), turn.

Row 2: *BPdc around 2nd dc of next fan, ch 2, sc in next dc, ch 2, BPdc around next dc, dc in next sc; rep from * across; ch 4 (counts as first dc and ch-1 sp on following row), turn.

Row 3: (Dc, ch 1, dc) in base of ch; *sc in next sc, work fan in next dc; rep from * across to last sc; sc in last sc, (dc, ch 1) twice in 3rd ch of turning ch, dc in same ch; ch 1, turn.

Row 4: Sc in first dc, ch 2, BPdc around next dc, dc in next sc; *BPdc around 2nd dc of next fan, ch 2, sc in next dc, ch 2, BPdc around next dc, dc in next sc; rep from * across, ending last rep with BPdc around last dc; ch 2, sc in 3rd ch of turning ch-4; ch 1, turn.

Row 5: Sc in first sc; *work fan in next dc, sc in next sc; rep from * across; ch 3, turn.

Repeat Rows 2 through 5 for pattern. At end of last row, do not ch or turn; finish off.

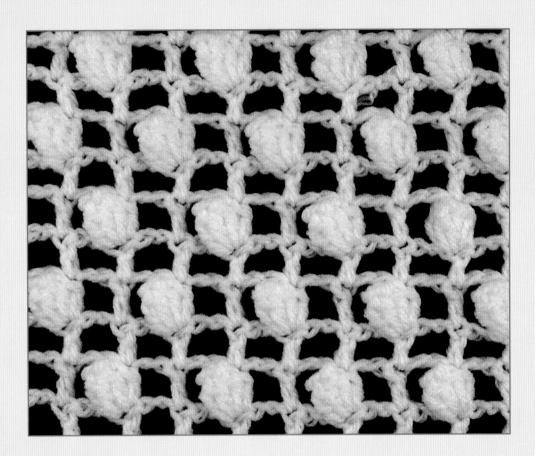

Filet Pops

Chain multiple: 3 + 1

Note: *Number of repeats must be uneven number.*

STITCH GUIDE

Popcorn (PC): Work 5 dc in specified st; drop lp from hook, insert hook from front to back through top of first dc made, insert hook in dropped lp and draw through lp on hook: PC made.

Instructions

Row 1 (right side): Sc in 2nd ch from hook and in each rem ch; ch 3 (counts as first dc on following rows), turn.

Row 2: Dc in next sc; *ch 2, skip next 2 sc, dc in next sc; rep from * to last sc; dc in last sc; ch 3, turn.

Row 3: *Dc in next dc, ch 2, PC in next dc; ch 2; rep from * to last dc and turning ch-3, dc in last dc, dc in 3rd ch of turning ch-3; ch 3, turn.

Row 4: Dc in next dc; *ch 2, dc in next PC, ch 2, dc in next dc; rep from * to turning ch-3; dc in 3rd ch of turning ch; ch 3, turn.

Row 5: Dc in next dc; *ch 2, dc in next dc, ch 2**; PC in next dc; rep from * across, ending last rep at **; dc in last dc, dc in 3rd ch of turning ch-3; ch 3, turn.

Row 6: *Dc in next dc, ch 2**, dc in next PC, ch 2; rep from * across, ending last rep at **; dc in last dc, dc in 3rd ch of turning ch-3; ch 3, turn.

Repeat Rows 3 through 6 for pattern. At end of last row, do not ch or turn; finish off.

Pop-Ups

Chain multiple: 6 + 2

STITCH GUIDE

Front Popcorn (FPc): 4 dc in specified st; remove hook from lp and insert it from front to back in first dc made; insert hook in dropped lp and draw through lp on hook, ch 1: FPc made.

Back Popcorn (BPc): 4 dc in specified st, remove hook from lp and insert it from back to front in first dc made; insert hook in dropped lp and draw through lp on hook, ch 1: BPc made.

Shell: Work 5 dc in specified st.

Instructions

Row 1: Sc in 2nd ch from hook and in each rem ch; ch 3 (counts as first dc of following rows), turn.

Row 2: 2 dc in first ch of turning ch-3, skip next 2 sc, FPc in next sc; *skip next 2 sc, shell in next sc; skip next 2 sc, FPc in next sc; rep from * to last 3 sc; skip next 2 sc, 3 dc in last sc; ch 1, turn.

Row 3: Sc in first dc, shell in ch-1 at top of next FPc; *BPc in 3rd dc of next shell, shell in ch-1 at top of next FPc; rep from * to last 3 sts; skip next 2 dc, sc in 3rd ch of turning ch-3; ch 3, turn.

Row 4: 2 dc in base of ch-3; FPc in 3rd dc of next shell; *shell in ch-1 at top of next BPc; FPc in 3rd dc of next shell; rep from * to last sc; 3 dc in last sc; ch 1, turn.

Rep Rows 3 and 4 for pattern. At end of last row, do not ch or turn; finish off.

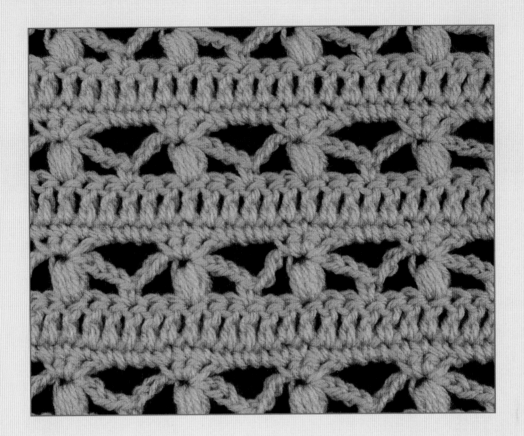

Puff Bridges

Chain multiple: 6 + 4

STITCH GUIDE

Puff St (PS): YO, insert hook in specified st and draw up a lp to height of a dc; (YO, insert hook in same st and draw up a lp to same height) 3 times; YO and draw through all 9 lps on hook; ch 1: PS made.

Instructions

Row 1 (right side): Sc in 2nd ch from hook and in each rem ch; ch 3 (counts as first dc of following rows), turn.

Row 2: Dc in each sc; ch 1, turn.

Row 3: Sc in each of first 2 dc; *loosely ch 3, skip next 2 dc, PS in next dc; loosely ch 3, skip next 2 dc, sc in next dc; rep from * across, sc in 3rd ch of turning ch-3; ch 5 (counts as first dc and ch-2 sp on following rows), turn.

Row 4: 3 sc in ch-1 at top of next PS; *ch 3, 3 sc in ch-1 at top of next PS; rep from * across to last 2 sc; ch 2, skip next sc, dc in last sc; ch 1, turn.

Row 5: Sc in first dc, 2 sc in next ch-2 sp; *sc in each of next 3 sc, 3 sc in next ch-3 sp; rep from * across, ending with sc in each of last 3 sc, 2 sc in next ch-5 sp, sc in 3rd ch of turning ch-5; ch 3, turn.

Repeat Rows 2 through 5 for pattern, ending with a Row 2. At end of last row, do not ch or turn; finish off.

Twin Puffs

Chain multiple: 8 + 5

STITCH GUIDE

Puff Stitch (PS): *YO, insert hook in specified ch or sp and draw up a lp to height of a dc; rep from * twice more in same st; YO and draw through all 7 lps: PS made.

Picot: Ch 3, sl st in base of ch: picot made.

Puff Stitch Shell (PS shell): Work (PS, picot, ch 3, PS, picot) in specified ch or sp: PS shell made.

Instructions

Row 1: Work PS shell in 9th ch from hook; ch 1, skip next 3 chs, dc in next ch; *ch 1, skip next 3 chs, PS shell in next ch; ch 1, skip next 3 chs, dc in next ch; rep from * across; ch 4 (counts as first dc and ch-1 sp on following row), turn.

Row 2: Work PS shell in ch-3 sp of next PS shell, ch 1, dc in next dc; *ch 1, work PS shell in ch-3 sp of next PS, ch 1, dc in next dc; rep from * across, ending last rep with dc in 3rd ch of beg 7 skipped chs; ch 4, turn.

Row 3: Work PS shell in ch-3 sp of next PS shell, ch 1, dc in next dc; *ch 1, work PS shell in ch-3 sp of next PS, ch 1, dc in next dc; rep from * across, ending last rep with dc in 3rd ch of turning ch-4; ch 4, turn.

Repeat Row 3 for pattern. At end of last row, do not ch or turn; finish off.

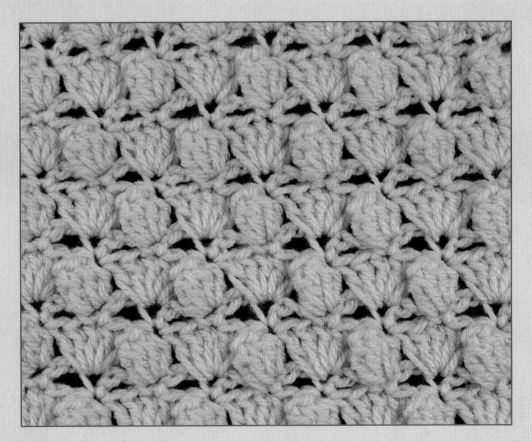

Sweet Popcorns and Shells

Chain multiple: 6 + 1

STITCH GUIDE

Shell: Work 5 dc in specified st: shell made.

Popcorn (PC): Work 5 dc in specified st; drop lp from hook, insert hook from front to back in top of first dc made, insert hook in dropped lp and draw through, ch 1: PC made.

Instructions

Row 1 (wrong side): Sc in 2nd ch from hook and in each rem ch; ch 3 (counts as first dc on following rows), turn.

Row 2 (right side): Skip first 2 sc; *shell in next sc, skip next 2 sc, PC in next sc, skip next 2 sc; rep from * to last 4 sc; shell in next sc, skip next 2 sc, dc in last sc; ch 3, turn.

Row 3: *Sc in 3rd dc of next shell, ch 2, sc in next PC, ch 2; rep from * across, ending last rep with sc in 3rd dc of last shell, ch 2, sc in 3rd ch of turning ch-3; ch 3, turn.

Row 4: *PC in next sc, shell in next sc; rep from * across, ending last rep with PC in next sc, ch 2, dc in base of turning ch-3; ch 3, turn.

Row 5: *Sc in next PC, ch 2, sc in 3rd dc of next shell, ch 2; rep from * across, ending last rep with sc in last PC, ch 2, dc in 3rd ch of turning ch-3; ch 3, turn.

Row 6: Shell in next sc; *PC in next sc, shell in next sc; rep from * across, ending last rep with dc in base of turning ch-3; ch 3, turn.

Repeat Rows 3 through 6 for pattern. At end of last row, do not ch or turn; finish off.

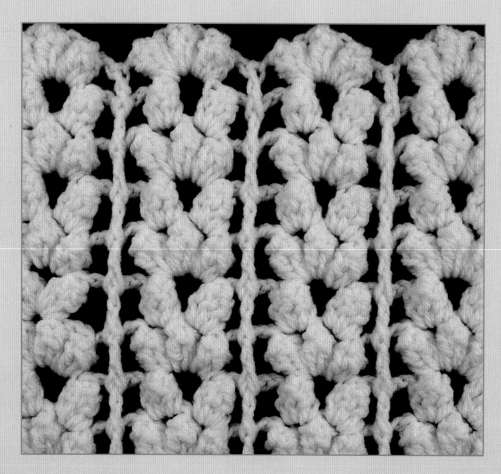

Bubbling Popcorns

Chain multiple: 6 + 2

STITCH GUIDE

Front Popcorn (FPc): Work 4 dc in specified st or sp; drop lp from hook, insert hook from front to back through top of first dc made, insert hook in dropped lp and draw it through lp on hook:FPc made.

Back Popcorn (BPc): Work 4 dc in specified st or sp; drop lp from hook, insert hook from back to front through top of first dc made, insert hook in dropped lp and draw it through lp on hook: BPc made.

Front post double crochet (FPdc): YO, insert hook from front to back to front around post (vertical bar) of specified st, YO and draw up a lp; (YO and draw through 2 lps) twice: FPdc made.

Back post double crochet (BPdc): YO, insert hook from back to front to back around post (vertical bar) of specified st, YO and draw up a lp; (YO and draw through 2 lps) twice: BPdc made.

Instructions

Row 1 (wrong side): Sc in 2nd ch from hook and in each rem ch; ch 5 (counts as first dc and ch-2 sp on following rows), turn.

Row 2 (right side): *Skip next 2 sc, work (FPc, ch 2, FPc, ch 2, FPc) in next sc; ch 2, skip next 2 sc, dc in next sc **; rep from * across, ending last rep at **; ch 5, turn.

Row 3: Skip first ch-2 sp; *BPc in next ch-2 sp, ch 3, BPc in next ch-2 sp, ch 2, BPdc around next dc, ch 2; rep from * across, ending last rep with dc in 3rd ch of turning ch-5; ch 5, turn.

Row 4: Work (FPc, ch 2, FPc, ch 2, FPc) in next ch-3 sp; ch 2, FPdc around next BPdc, ch 2; rep from * across, ending last rep with dc in 3rd ch of turning ch-5; ch 5, turn.

Repeat Rows 3 and 4 for pattern. At end of last row, do not ch or turn; finish off.

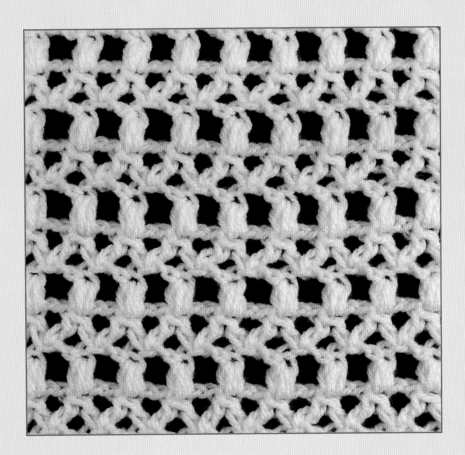

Delicate Puffs

Chain multiple: 3

STITCH GUIDE

Puff St (PS): (YO, insert hook in specified st and draw up a lp to height of a dc) 3 times; YO and draw through all 7 lps on hook, ch 1: PS made.

Dc decrease (dc dec): YO, insert hook in first specified st or sp and draw up a lp, YO and draw through 2 lps on hook, YO, insert hook in second specified st or sp and draw up a lp, YO and draw through 2 lps on hook; YO and draw through all 3 lps on hook: dc dec made.

Instructions

Row 1 (right side): Dc in 6th ch from hook, ch 2, dc dec in same ch as last dc made and in 3rd ch (skipping 2 chs between); *ch 2, dc dec in same ch as 2nd half of last dc dec made and in 3rd ch (skipping 2 chs between); rep from * across; ch 1, dc in same ch as second half of last dc dec; ch 4 (counts as first dc and ch-1 sp on following row), turn.

Row 2: Puff st in first dc dec; *ch 3, puff st in next dc dec; rep from * to last dc; ch 3, skip last dc, dc in turning ch; ch 3, turn.

Row 3: Dc in 2nd ch of next ch-3 sp, ch 2, dc dec in same ch as last dc made and in 2nd ch of next ch-3 sp; *ch 2, dc dec in same ch as second half of last dc dec made and in 2nd ch of next ch-3 sp; rep from * across, working second half of last dc dec in 3rd ch of turning ch-4; ch 1, dc in same ch as second half of last dc dec; ch 4, turn.

Repeat Rows 2 and 3 for pattern. At end of last row, do not ch or turn; finsh off.

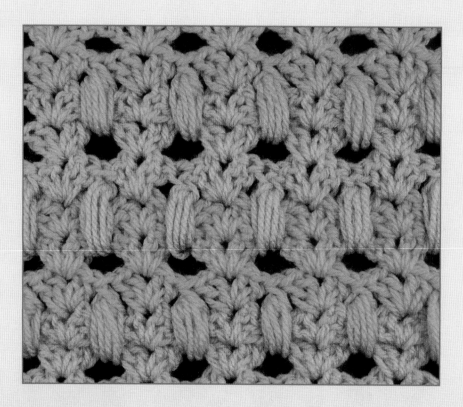

Shells and Puffs

Chain multiple: 4 + 6

Two colors: color A and color B

STITCH GUIDE

Shell: (2 dc, ch 1, 2 dc) in specified st or sp: shell made.

Puff Stitch (Pst): (YO, insert hook in sp before first shell in 2nd row below and draw up a lp to height of working row) 4 times: 9 lps on hook: YO and draw through first 8 lps on hook, YO and draw through remaining 2 lps: Pst made.

Instructions

Note: *Work beg chain with color A.*

Row 1 (right side): With color A, dc in 4th ch from hook (beg 3 skipped chs count as a dc) and in next ch; *skip next 2 chs, 2 dc in next ch, ch 1, 2 dc in next ch; rep from * to last 5 chs; sk next 2 chs, dc in each of last 3 chs; ch 3 (counts as first dc on following rows), turn.

Row 2: Dc in each of next 2 dc; *work shell in next ch-1 sp; repeat from * to last 3 sts; dc in each of next 2 dc, dc in 3rd ch of turning ch-3; change to color B, ch 3, turn.

Row 3: With new color, dc in each of next 2 dc; Pst in sp before first shell in 2nd row below; *shell in ch-1 sp of next shell, Pst in next ch-1 sp between shells on 2nd row below; rep from * to last shell; shell in ch-1 sp of last shell, Pst in ch-1 sp before last shell on 2nd row below; dc in next 2 dc, dc in 3rd ch of turning ch-3; ch 3, turn.

Row 4: Dc in each of next 2 dc; *skip next Pst, shell in ch-1 sp of next shell; rep from * to last Pst; skip last Pst, dc in each of next 2 dc, dc in 3rd ch of turning ch-3; ch 3, turn.

Row 5: Rep Row 2, changing colors in last dc.

Rows 6 and 7: Rep Rows 3 and 4.

Row 8: Dc in each of next 2 dc; *shell in next ch-1 sp; rep from * to last 3 sts; dc in each of next 2 dc, dc in 3rd ch of turning ch-3; change to next color; ch 3, turn.

Repeat Rows 6 through 8 for pattern. At end of last row, do not ch or turn; finish off.

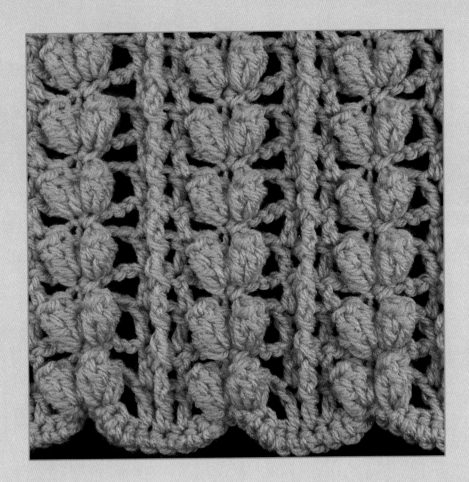

Popcorns and Posts

Chain multiple: 10 + 4

STITCH GUIDE

Popcorn (PC): Work 5 dc in specified st; drop lp from hook, insert hook from front to back in top of first dc made; insert hook in dropped lp and draw lp through; ch 1: PC made.

Front post triple crochet (FPtr): YO twice; insert hook from front to back to front around post (vertical post) of specified st; (YO and draw through 2 lps) 3 times: FPtr made.

Back post triple crochet (BPtr): YO twice; insert hook from back to front to back post (vertical post) of specified st; (YO and draw through 2 lps) 3 times: BPtr made.

Instructions

Row 1 (wrong side): Sc in 2nd ch from hook and in each rem ch; ch 3 (counts as first dc on following rows), turn.

Row 2 (right side): Dc in each of next 2 sc; *ch 2, skip next 3 sc, (PC in next sc, ch 1) twice; skip next 2 sc, dc in each of next 3 sc; rep from * across; ch 3, turn.

Row 3: BPtr around next st, dc in next st; *ch 3, sk next ch and next PC, 2 sc in next ch-1 sp; ch 3, skip next PC and next ch-2 sp, dc in next st, BPtr around next st, dc in next st; rep from * across, ending last rep with dc in 3rd ch of turning ch-3; ch 3, turn.

Row 4: FPtr around next st, dc in next st; *ch 2, skip next ch-3 sp, (PC in next sc, ch 1) twice; skip next ch-3 sp, dc in next st, FPtr around next st, dc in next st; rep from * across, ending last rep with dc in 3rd ch of turning ch-3; ch 3, turn.

Repeat Rows 3 and 4 for pattern. At end of last row, do not ch or turn; finish off.

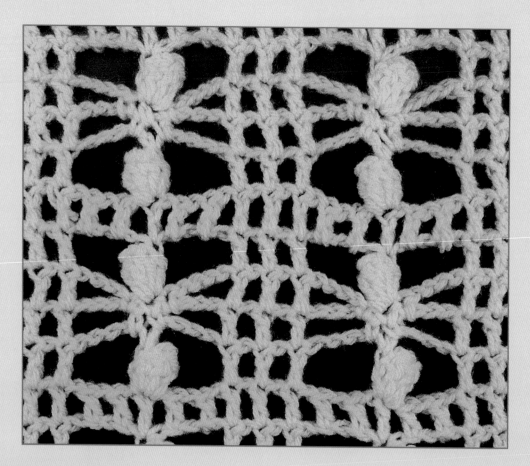

Popcorn Columns

Chain multiple: 16 + 8

STITCH GUIDE

Front Popcorn (FPc): Work 5 dc in specified st or sp; drop lp from hook, insert hook from front to back through top of first dc made, insert hook in dropped lp and draw through: FPc made.

Back Popcorn (BPc): Work 5 dc in specified st or sp; drop lp from hook, insert hook from back to front through top of first dc made, insert hook in dropped lp and draw through: BPc made.

Instructions

Row 1 (wrong side): Dc in 6th ch from hook (5 skipped chs count as first dc, ch-1 sp and dc); *ch 1, skip next ch, dc in next ch; rep from* across; ch 4 (counts as first dc and ch-1 sp on following rows), turn.

Row 2 (right side): Dc in next dc, ch 1, dc in next dc; *ch 5, skip next 2 dc, FPc in next dc; ch 5, skip next 2 dc, dc in next dc, (ch 1, dc in next dc) twice; rep from * across, ending last rep with dc in 3rd ch of beg 5 skipped chs; ch 4 (counts as first dc and ch-1 sp on following rows), turn.

Row 3: Dc in next dc, ch 1, dc in next dc; *ch 4, sc in next ch-5 sp, skip next FPc, sc in next ch-5 sp, ch 4, dc in next dc, (ch 1, skip next ch-1 sp, dc in next st) twice; rep from * across, ending last rep with dc in 3rd ch of turning ch-4; ch 4, turn.

Row 4: Dc in next dc, ch 1, dc in next dc; *ch 4, sc in next ch-4 sp, sc between next 2 sc, sc in next ch-4 sp; ch 4, dc in next dc, (ch 1, skip next ch-1 sp, dc in next st) twice; rep from * across, ending last rep with dc in 3rd ch of turning ch-4; ch 4, turn.

Row 5: Dc in next dc, ch 1, dc in next dc; *ch 5, BPc in 2nd of next 3 sc, ch 5, dc in next dc, (ch 1, dc in next st) twice; rep from * across, ending last rep with dc in 3rd ch of turning ch-4; ch 4, turn.

Row 6: (Dc in next dc, ch 1) twice, *(dc, ch 1) twice over next ch-5, dc in BPc, (ch 1, dc) twice over next ch-5 **(ch 1, dc in next dc) 3 times, ch 1; rep from * across, ending last rep at **, ch 1, dc next dc, ch 1, dc in 3rd ch of turning ch-4.

Repeat Rows 2 through 6 for pattern, alternating FPcs and BPcs as needed to maintain pattern. At end of last row, do not ch or turn; finish off.

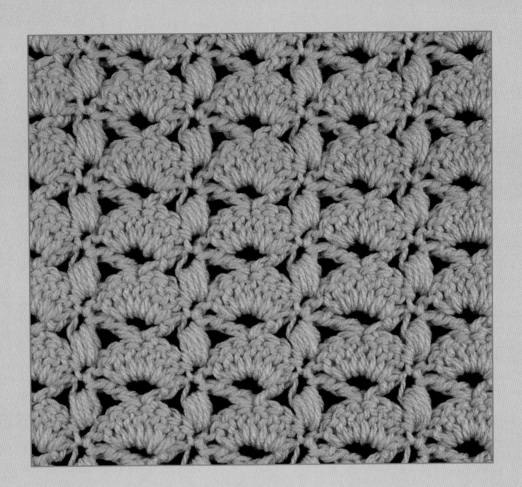

Linked Puffs and Shells

Chain multiple: 6 + 4

STITCH GUIDE

Puff Stitch (Pst): (YO, insert hook in specified st and draw up a lp to height of a dc) 4 times; YO and draw through all 9 lps, ch 1: Pst made.

Shell: Work 7 dc in specified sp: shell made

Instructions

Row 1 (right side): Sc in 2nd ch from hook and in each rem ch; ch 3 (counts as first dc on following rows), turn.

Row 2: Dc in next sc; *skip next 2 sc, work (dc, ch 3, dc) in next sc, skip next 2 sc, Pst in next sc; rep from *to last 7 sc; skip next 2 sc, work (dc, ch 3, dc) in next sc, skip next 2 sc, dc in each of last 2 sc; ch 3, turn.

Row 3: Dc in next dc; *shell in next ch-3 sp, sc in next Pst; rep from * to last ch-3 sp; shell in last ch-3 sp, dc in next dc, dc in 3rd ch of turning ch-3; ch 3, turn.

Row 4: Dc in next dc; *work (dc, ch 3, dc) in 4th dc of next shell, Pst in next sc; rep from * across to last shell; work (dc, ch 3, dc) in 4th dc of last shell, dc in last dc, dc in 3rd ch of turning ch-3; ch 3, turn.

Repeat Rows 3 and 4 for pattern, ending with a Row 3. At end of last row, do not ch or turn; finish off.

General Directions

ABBREVIATIONS AND SYMBOLS

Crochet patterns are written in a special shorthand which is used so that instructions don't take up too much space. They sometimes seem confusing, but once you learn them, you'll have no trouble following them.

These are Standard Abbreviations

BB	Bobble
BBcl	Bobble cluster
Beg	beginning
BL	back loop
BPc	back popcorn
BPdc	back post double crochet
BPsc	back post single crochet
BPtr	back post triple crochet
BS	basket stitch
Cl(s)	cluster(s)
Ch(s)	chain(s)
Cont	continue
Dc	double crochet
Dc Cl	double crochet cluster
Dc dec	double crochet decrease
Dc inc	double crochet increase
Dec	decrease
Dtr Cl	double triple crochet cluster
Dtr	double triple crochet
Fig	figure
FL	front loop
Fpc	front popcorn
FPdc	front post double crochet
FPsc	front post single crochet
FPtr	front post triple crochet
Hdc	half double crochet
Inc	Increase(ing)
Lp(s)	loop(s)
Patt	pattern
PC	popcorn
Prev	previous
PS	puff stitch
Rem	remaining
Rep	repeat(ing)
Rnd(s)	round(s)
Sc	single crochet
Sc dec	single crochet decrease
Sc2tog	single crochet 3 stitches together decrease
SK	skip
Sl st	slip stitch
Sp(s)	space(s)
St(s)	stitch(es)
Tog	together
Tr	triple crochet
V-st	V-stitch
YO	yarn over hook
Y-st	Y-stitch

These are Standard Symbols

*An asterisk (or double asterisks**) in a pattern row, indicates a portion of instructions to be used more than once. For instance, "rep from * three times" means that after working the instructions once, you must work them again three times for a total of 4 times in all.

†A dagger (or double daggers ††) indicates that those instructions will be repeated again later in the same row or round.

: The number of stitches after a colon tells you the number of stitches you will have when you have completed the row or round.

( ) Parentheses enclose instructions which are to be worked the number of times following the parentheses. For instance, "(ch 1, sc, ch1) 3 times" means that you will chain one, work one sc, and then chain again three times for a total of six chains and three scs. Parentheses often set off or clarify a group of stitches to be worked into the same space of stitch. For instance, "(dc, ch2, dc) in corner sp".

[ ] Brackets and ( ) parentheses are also used to give you additional information.

Terms

Front Loop – This is the loop toward you at the top of the crochet stitch.

Back Loop – This is the loop away from you at the top of the crochet stitch.

Post – This is the vertical part of the crochet stitch

Join – This means to join with a sl st unless another stitch is specified.

Finish Off – This means to end your piece by pulling the cut yarn end through the last loop remaining on the hook. This will prevent the work from unraveling.

Crochet Terminology

The patterns in this book have been written using the crochet terminology that is used in the United States. Terms which may have different equivalents in other parts of the world are listed below.

United States	International
Double crochet (dc)	treble crochet (tr)
Gauge	tension
Half double crochet (hdc)	half treble crochet (htr)
Single crochet	double crochet
Skip	miss
Slip stitch	single crochet
Triple crochet (tr)	double treble crochet (dtr)
Yarn over (YO)	yarn forward (yfwd)